Black Eye
and Other Short Plays

By
Carolyn Gage

Praise for Carolyn Gage's plays:

"Carolyn Gage is one of the best lesbian playwrights in America..."—*Lambda Book Report*, Los Angeles.

"The culture of women we have never had is invented in Carolyn Gage's brilliant and beautiful plays."—Andrea Dworkin, feminist philosopher activist, and author.

"The work of an experienced and esteemed playwright like Carolyn Gage is the air that modern theatre needs."—Jewelle Gomez, author of *The Gilda Stories*, San Francisco Arts Commissioner.

"Gage's dramatic and lesbian imagination is utterly original... daring, heartbreaking, principled, bitter, and often very funny... There is no rhetoric here: only one swift and pleasurable intake of breath after another... Women's mental health would improve, instantly, were they able to read and see these plays performed."—Phyllis Chesler, author of *Women and Madness*.

"Ever since I first saw Carolyn Gage perform her work, I have been convinced that she is one of our greatest living artists... Gage creates plays that bring the "magic" back to theatre. The impact of these performances on audiences is profound and life-changing."—Dr. Morgne Cramer, Dept. of English, University of Connecticut, Stamford.

"Carolyn Gage's writing, acting, and teaching are explosive. She rips away the cultural camouflage that permits us to accept, to be blind to, the brutal context in which women are still required to live their lives... "—Prof. George Wolf, Dept. of English, University of Nebraska, Lincoln.

"No playwright has created as amazing a pantheon of historical lesbian characters... Carolyn Gage is a national lesbian treasure."—Rosemary Keefe Curb, editor of *Amazon All Stars : 13 Lesbian Plays*.

"Rarely in my life have I left a play, or any work of art, feeling like my life was truly better for it... The plays were hilarious, harrowing, exhilarating, and affirming."—*The Spectrum*, Buffalo, NY.

"Taking in a Gage play is like getting a combined dose of Karl Marx, Betty Friedan and triple espresso. She broadcasts insight on power and powerlessness with energetic zip, laying good groundwork for directors and actors who would attempt production of them."—WNYQ News, Buffalo, NY.

v

Other Books by Carolyn Gage

Three Comedies

Starting from Zero: Short Plays About Lesbians in Love

The Triple Goddess: Three Plays

The Gaia Papers: In Search of a Science of Gaia

The Spindle and Other Lesbian Fairy Tales

The Second Coming of Joan of Arc and Selected Plays (2008)

Nine Short Plays

Monologues and Scenes for Lesbian Actors: Revised and Expanded

Sermons for a Lesbian Tent Revival

Take Stage! How to Direct and Produce a Lesbian Play

*Like There's No Tomorrow: Meditations for Women
Leaving Patriarchy*

The Second Coming of Joan of Arc and Other Plays (1994)

Black Eye and Other Short Plays

Table of Contents

Black Eye and Other Short Plays

Introduction

This is a collection of short plays with strong social critiques, including critiques of war (and peacekeeping efforts), gender roles, heterosexuality, post-structuralism, and surrogacy. The plays are highly compressed and include two five-minute plays.

Black Eye

This play was written in response to an intriguing call for short plays based on the subjects in Norman Rockwell's *Saturday Evening Post* covers. Looking through the possible subjects, I was struck by the painting titled *The Girl with the Black Eye*, dated 1953.

The painting of a jubilant tomgirl with the black eye waiting outside the principal's office was interesting to me for several reasons: First, I am a lesbian and a fighter. Second, I was born in 1952. Third, Rockwell's depiction of the adults, seen through a crack in the office door, fascinated me. He shows a perplexed, somewhat bookish principal seated at his desk, with a tall woman leaning on her arm and towering over him. The woman's hair is very short and she appears to be asserting herself. There is a half-smile on her face.

The Girl with the Black Eye could be seen as an amusing and harmless reversal of gender roles, except for his unusual choice regarding the adults. There is an adult female of somewhat ambiguous gender presentation in a position of physical dominance over the male authority figure.

In 1953, the first of the *Kinsey Reports* was beginning to rock the country with its revelations about human sexuality. Not only were most married couples adulterous, but also—according to Kinsey—one-out-of-ten men and women were reporting experiences with same-sex intimacy. Homosexuality was far more common than previously believed, and apparently a normal variant of human sexuality.

Although often considered emblematic of "the American Dream," Norman Rockwell's illustrations are not always idyllic, as with his depiction of one of the Little Rock Nine, being escorted by the National Guard to her classroom. Like Thornton Wilder's play *Our Town*, the cracks in the façade are visible if one looks closely.

The 1950's were an era of violent enforcement of Jim Crow segregation in the South and rigid housing and educational apartheid in other areas of the country. It was also a decade of Communist witch-hunts, which had become conflated with homophobic witch-hunting, because the federal government had historically been a safe haven for gay and lesbian workers. McCarthyites exposed and exploited this fact to further their agenda, hence the term "pinko Commie."

It was also an era when sexual harassment in the workplace and at school was rampant, unchecked by legislation such as we have today. Young women find it difficult to believe that there was a time when male bosses could, with impunity, touch their employees on the breasts, pat us on our backsides, and make indecent proposals and suggestive remarks, or tell dirty jokes any time they wanted. Studies of that era show that eighty-five percent of women changed jobs because of sexual harassment, and many changed them more than once. These disrupted job histories were serious handicaps for women attempting to build careers. Also women were paid far less than men and denied advancement, with no legal recourse. Rape was considered rare, and reports of rape were dismissed as acts of vindictiveness on the part of women. There were no rape crisis lines or rape advocates, and reporting rape to all-male police teams became a second ordeal. Lesbians and women of color reporting rapes were often at risk of being raped again, this time by the police. Rape in marriage was completely legal. If a rape case made it to trial, the victim's entire sexual history was considered fair game, and she was likely to be humiliated and scapegoated if she testified. The majority chose to suffer in silence.

Also birth control and abortion were illegal. Young women walked an impossible line between being shunned as prudes or lesbians, and the lifelong disgrace of an out-of-wedlock pregnancy—or the misery of a loveless marriage for the sake of appearances.

Alcoholics Anonymous was still in its infancy, and alcoholism was rampant, with the violence and destruction that accompany the disease. Friends *did* let friends drink and drive, and, moreover, there was an epidemic of denial about what is now termed "domestic violence." There were no battered women's shelters, and divorced women were deeply stigmatized. Child sexual abuse went unreported, and the old Freudian notion of the promiscuous child was prevalent, discouraging survivors from coming forward.

I felt that *Girl with the Black Eye* was a commentary on conditions for women. More than that, Rockwell was celebrating the girl who would not put up with it, the girl who fought back, who took her lumps, and who was proud of standing up for herself. He also suggests the presence of the adult female ally—foreshadowing the tidal wave of feminist activism that was about to break over the country, changing the world forever.

I was also interested in exploring the relative positions of a closeted gay man and a closeted lesbian, both working within the system. It has been my experience, after two decades of lesbian activism, that gay men have more access to mainstream privilege, and, because of this, there are often painful limits to their participation in coalition causes, especially those involving advocacy for women's issues and for children's rights. The so-called effeminate man and the so-called masculine women face similar and dissimilar oppressions, and because of this, we often evolve oppositional strategies for surviving in a heterosexist world. I wanted to explore how that would play out in a harassment scenario where the mainstream was protecting male dominant behavior with a credo of "boys will be boys."

I believe in fighting, and I believe in teaching children, and especially girls, to defend themselves—verbally and physically. I share Rockwell's celebration of the tomboy, and it was a challenge to create a dramatic vignette as tight, as neatly encapsulated as a Norman Rockwell painting.

The Ladies' Room

The bathroom has been a site of "gender anxiety" historically, as well as a battlefield, and, although it is tempting to write this off to ignorance about gender and fanatical, knee-jerk policing of the "gender binary," the issue goes deeper than this.

Rapists do choose public bathrooms as sites of sexual predation, and the presence of men in traditionally female spaces is often dangerous. At the same time, transgender women and masculine women are harassed and humiliated when we attempt to use public facilities. What is the "politically correct" attitude toward gender presentation, when the ability to identify a stranger's biological sex in an isolated environment can be a question of life or death? And is that a problem that the woman who is being challenged or harassed needs to take on?

The A-Mazing Yamashita and the Millennnial Gold Diggers

I wanted to write a play about pornography and prostitution, but I wanted this play to do more than preach to the choir. I wanted a play that did more than make the point, "These things are bad for women." I wanted to write a play that illustrated the ways in which prostituted women are seasoned and witnesses become confused, then passive, then complicit. Pornography and prostitution do not occur in a vacuum. They occur in a context, and that context, although centuries old, is, like the cells of our bodies, also constantly renewing itself.

Each generation and each individual replicates the conditions that support both, in tiny reactions and interactions that occur in consciousness, minute by minute. I wanted to exploit that process in my audience by taking advantage of the social pressures on a theatre audience, leading them down that slippery slope of consensus until they realize with a shock that they have become participants in generating the context for perpetration.

I had been reading about General Yamashita, who, according to legend hid a stolen fortune in tunnels under a mountain and then blew up the entrances, sealing the workers inside. This seemed like a metaphor for what patriarchy does to women—first stealing our sense of who we are by erasing our history, our spirituality, our art—and then disguising the mechanisms by which our treasures have been buried and our witnesses silenced.

The play is presented as a magic show, because the conventions of magic suited perfectly my purposes. It is the audience's trained responses, their expectations about reality, which prevent them from seeing what is really happening. As the magician directs our attention to one hand, it is the other that is busy with the mechanics behind the illusion. Yamashita plays on the audience's understanding that they are at an entertainment (the expectation with both pornography and prostitution) in order to perpetrate.

Thinking of traditional magician tricks, I chose three that would be metaphors for the degradation of women: levitation, cutting a woman in half, and disappearing a woman in a box.

The levitation would illustrate the pressures on women to take anti-depressants, to drink, and so on. The codes of patriarchy dictate that women as caregivers and sex objects have no business being depressed, because being a "downer" takes the focus off those we are supposed to be servicing, drawing attention to our own unmet needs. Women's depression, now global and epidemic, is seen as a pathology instead of a symptom of a global economic, political, biological, and spiritual catastrophe. "Just take that pill, honey…"

The business of cutting a woman in two was fascinating to me, because the severance traditionally occurs at the waist —in other words, the woman's genitalia become disconnected from her brain and heart. This is a perfect description of a type of dissociation that is prevalent among populations of women who have been sexually violated.

Finally, the act of causing women to disappear spoke to the documented disappearance of more than a hundred million women every year—from female infanticide, the brutality of the sex trade, disproportionate neglect, "honor" killings, "dowry deaths," domestic violence, unsafe childbirth, and genital mutilation.

In researching *Yamashita*, I read many articles on economics, including the work of Marilyn Waring and also the radical work by writers like Butch Lee. I began to make connections between how pornography makes inequality appear sexy, and how capitalism is fuelled by inequality. Putting this together with studies about the brain, how synaptic connections in the brain can be made simply by causing neurons to fire simultaneously, and how easy it is for the brain to confuse the arousal of fear with the arousal of attraction. Having read extensively about Stockholm Syndrome and having witnessed it up-close and personal for eighteen years (my mother), I began to feel that magician's tricks were not just a metaphor but also a reality in the programming of entire cultures.

It was my friend Melissa Farley's suggestion that I include an exposé of how post-modern theory has been used to impede feminist activism, occupying itself with linguistic sleight-of-hand to "deconstruct" identities in lieu of offering strategies and tools for confronting oppression.

It was my intention to script a play that would have an effect like Clifford Odets' classic short play, *Waiting for Lefty*, which ends with a powerful collective call for a union strike. As the actors shout the final lines, "Strike! Strike!" whole audiences were said to have risen, fists pumping in the air, as they joined their voices to those of the actors.

I wanted to write a play then would end with a collective audience epiphany about the manipulation that was being practiced on them and that would trigger a repudiation of the global hocus-pocus that is disappearing both women's productivity and women and girls themselves. *The A-Mazing Yamashita* is intended to unmask the connections between pornography and prostitution, and how both of them enable finance capitalism.

The Rules of the Playground

The Rules of the Playground is a play about the gendered nature of violence, and especially of war. More than that, it is a play about women's denial of this, and our subsequent complicity in the atrocities perpetrated in the name of national security or religious freedom. I wrote it on the eve of the United States' invasion of Iraq.

In the play, the women—all mothers—have come together for a workshop as part of a program sponsored by their children's middle school—a program to eliminate violence in the schools. The program has been designed by so-called experts on global violence. The trainers are analysts from international "think tanks" and peacekeeping organizations. The one thing these pundits never do is analyze or confront acts of war as unacceptable male behaviors. It was my intention to demonstrate that this disguising and protecting of violence as a male prerogative is, in fact, the true agenda behind contemporary, mainstream political analyses.

Thirty years after the Second Wave of women's liberation, we still fail to organize collectively outside of left-wing, male-dominated, ineffectual peace movements, to oppose war as a phenomenon perpetrated by men, serving many of their interests at the expense of women and children. To suggest such a thing is to invite dismissal as a tunnel-visioned, reductionist, somewhat simple-minded holdover from 1970's feminism.

Intelligent women give our precious energy to studying and analyzing the most criminal atrocities as the "natural," "tragic," or "inevitable" results of boundary disputes, ideological conflicts, ethnic and/or religious differences. War is defined in terms of "human nature," never in terms of "male behavior." We are complicit with apparently well-intended efforts of "peacekeepers" to monitor and adjudicate atrocity, in lieu of responding with moral outrage. We buy into the media's categorizing of atrocities committed by "us" as "collateral damages," the result of "necessary targets," and their labeling of atrocities by "them" as acts of terrorism.

In writing *Rules of the* Playground, I looked to Shirley Jackson's unforgettable short story, "The Lottery" for a model. In her story, a ritual atrocity has become "normalized" in the life of a contemporary, small New England town. It is this normalization that is the source of the reader's horror.

In the play, the women have been persuaded that their former approach to playground violence—the use of "timeouts"—is a form of scapegoating that will perpetuate violence. In fact, the "timeout," in which the child is socially isolated for a period of time, is a humane, appropriate, efficient, and effective con-sequence of indulging in anti-social behavior. Instead of trusting their own judgment, the women are being taught to listen to the experts, and refocus on an obsessive and impossible quest for absolute equality via an ongoing, obsessive remapping of the playground.

The windows are covered, and the mothers are prevented from observing the behaviors of their children on the playground, as this might elicit a too-subjective response to the violence. Women are encouraged by the media to ignore the gendered nature of military violence, adopting male-protectionist analyses that blind us to the true nature and individual motives behind these collective male acts.

In *The Rules of the Playground,* the original women in the workshop are named after famous female political leaders who identified themselves with male-dominated political parties. Shelley, the newcomer, is the only one not so-named, and also the only one to challenge the insanity of the brainwashing that is going on.

I wanted to show the ways in which women train each other to enable male violence through censorship of ourselves, intentional disabling of our powers of observation, and a grotesque enthusiasm for methodologies specifically designed to perpetuate the violence. Conspicuous in its absence is any official and substantive political analysis of the condition of women—a sure indication that women are being recruited to participate in our own oppression.

Finally, I wanted to make the point that it is the women who have experienced the most serious losses who become the self-appointed enforcers of the program. In the play the motives for Jeanne and Madeleine's actions at the end are ambiguous. Certainly, they actively intervene to suppress a potential for resistance, but do they do it in order to justify their own losses, to have the other women experience similar losses, or in some wild hope that the separate space they crave will eventually emerge from an all-out war of mutually assured male destruction?

The women are susceptible to brainwashing, because of their awe of the credentials of the male-identified experts. They are easily shamed about the methods and philosophies they have evolved in the gynocentric field of childcare. They are quick to concur with the trainers that a subjective, emotional response to violence is undesirable, that actual observation of a behavior *as a behavior* is a distraction. But are the women really this gullible? Might it not be that their compliant transfer of focus to the rules of the playground is *their* gendered expression of violence?

The Boundary Trial of John Proctor

The Boundary Trial of John Proctor was the first radical feminist play I ever wrote, and it reflects the major influences on me at the time.

This was my first use of the circle. I would use circles again, later, in *Heterosexuals Anonymous, The Drum Lesson,* and *Esther and Vashti.* It's interesting to me to trace the evolution of my circles, because they mirror the evolution of my consciousness of feminist community and place. This circle is a circle of traditional women, but still in reference to a man. This circle holds John Proctor's wife, his mistress, a neighbor's servant, and the women in his village who were also hanged. The have come together ostensibly to practice the domestic arts (and teach them to Proctor!), but subversion of the traditional gender roles and stereotypes is the subtext. The famous tee shirt of the 1970's, with the logo "Ladies Sewing Circle and Terrorist Society," is modeled in this *Crucible* circle. They use the knitting to intimidate and discipline Proctor. They do not resemble their former incarnations, and Proctor has difficulty identifying them. And, finally, they collapse the circle in order to create or take their places in a larger one that is not seen on the stage.

The women in Miller's play represent stock archetypes in the patriarchal drama: the frigid wife counterposed to the slutty mistress, the raving bag lady counterposed to the saintly grandmother, the bluestocking intellectual counterposed to the superstitious native. I needed for Miller's characters to put his alter-ego on trial, but I did not want to validate or even replicate these offensive stereotypes, and so I structured the play somewhat unusually: The cast list specifies that the women may be of any age, any race, any ethnicity. Within the play, it is evident that neither Abigail nor Elizabeth is the age of their characters in the play. Neither do their personalities reflect those of the Miller characters. In terms of play structure, the women act as one character, which is another reason I did not individuate them with personalities, or even particularly divergent points of view. This may have also been a reflection of my naïveté in 1986, before I had really begun my journey into communities of women, when I still cherished a dream of universal sisterhood that was more based on illusions of homogeneity, instead of true diversity.

The concept of a boundary space between patriarchy and woman-identified territory came from the writings of Mary Daly, major influences on me during this period. I chose *The Crucible*, because it is a classic in the

Western canon (it had been my directing class text) and because it deals with witches and witch trials. (I was also reading Sonia Johnson's *Housewife to Heretic* at this time!) John Proctor is a typical male, liberal protagonist whose privilege and gender-role assumptions are more-or-less intact.

Proctor is confronted by a circle of women apparently bonded by their domestic responsibilities—foremost, their care of children. He is ordered to knit a sweater for his unborn child. The work is monotonous, but a task that requires the knitter's complete attention. Work done poorly must be pulled out and done over. As noted earlier, Proctor cannot identify the women. Either their appearances have undergone radical transformation, or he had never experienced their authentic selves. Failing to identify them, Proctor *refuses* to recognize them (a recurrent theme in my work), chafes at the mundane drudgery, and arrogantly rejects the authority of the circle and their self-identification as witches.

The ending of the play is a tribute to the Marlene Gorris film, *A Question of Silence*—also a major influence in my transition across the boundary. In this film, three women who are strangers to each other happen to be in a clothing boutique at the same time, when one of them is apprehended shoplifting and subsequently humiliated by the male store manager. The women spontaneously murder him. None of the many female shoppers in the store who witnessed the murder come forward to testify, but they appear in the courtroom as spectators in a show of solidarity for the defendants.

The pivotal character is the psychiatrist who has been hired to determine their sanity. As she works with the women, she becomes more and more convinced that this seemingly senseless personal action was an act of war and that there is nothing wrong with the women. As I remember, at the end of the film, one of the male attorneys asserts that the women had no motive for what they did. At this point, the defendants begin to laugh. The laughter spreads to the silent witnesses in the courtroom, and finally to the psychiatrist herself. All of the women are laughing at the men, at their courts, their laws, their arrogance, their utter ignorance about themselves and about the truth of women's lives, and their stupidity. They begin a mass exodus from the courtroom.

These women have stopped arguing, reasoning, petitioning. They are simply laughing and walking out. It was an astonishing moment.

After Proctor has left the stage, the women begin to laugh. They throw down their knitting, which they previously characterized as work integral to their identities and missions in life. It was my intention for the audience to understand that the knitting circle was staged by these women for the sole purpose of confronting Proctor and tricking him into walking out on them, into that boundary space that would spell existential annihilation for him.

This shift from the patriarchal view of boundary space to the matriarchal is also reflected in my use of the word "witch." From Proctor's point of view, they are witches, because they do not respond to acts or threats of violence—something that can only be perceived by him as supernatural and evil. From the women's point of view, using Proctor's definition of a witch as a woman who traffics with the devil, the real witches are the women who collaborate with the patriarchy. Finally, in a matriarchal reclamation of the term, the women at the end of the play, throwing off even the costumes and roles of patriarchy, are witches in the sense of wild and undomesticated, filled with gynergetic, symbiotic potential.

Does such a boundary really exist, or did Proctor call their bluff? Are the women mocking the conventions of traditional domesticity, mirroring Proctor's attitudes toward "women's work," or do they really mean what they say? When they throw down the knitting and break up the circle, who do they become? Are they real witches?

The Evil That Men Do: The Story of Thalidomide

Female mentoring is a well-kept secret in patriarchy, but it exists, and where it does, it is very powerful. Mainstream cultural representations of women in the workplace tend to indulge in titillating scenarios of catfights between women, or unrealistic portrayals of a superwoman acting in a kind of social vacuum devoid of any friendships or alliances with other women.

When I read the story of Dr. Francis Kelsey (in a collection of stories about powerful women written by Margaret Truman), I immediately wanted to write a play about her successful fight against the Food and Drug Administration (FDA). I was attracted to her story, of course, because it was a tale of one woman who faced down an entire governmental agency and who saved thousands of women from the agony of giving birth to children with severe birth defects. I was intrigued by this woman, who, a decade before the Women's Liberation Movement, made an issue about the lack of medical testing of drugs on females and fetuses, insisting that our very different biology, including our reproductive capacities, warranted special attention.

But I was also intrigued by her friendship with Dr. Barbara Moulton, a whistleblower at the FDA who, at the time when Dr. Kelsey was hired, was testifying before the Senate about the connections between drug companies and the FDA. An ambitious woman might think twice about befriending a female troublemaker who is being scapegoated out of the agency where she herself just got hired, especially when that agency is predominantly male. Dr. Kelsey made an unusual choice: She befriended Dr. Moulton and attended the hearings. She actually wanted to hear Moulton's charges of corruption. Moulton became her mentor, explaining the manipulative techniques that the drug companies had developed for alternately bullying and bribing doctors to approve new drugs without adequate testing. Because of this mentoring, Kelsey was prepared for her ordeal.

Many women have trouble standing up for ourselves in the face of institutional male power. We have been taught to question our judgment and to doubt our perceptions. In *The Evil That Men Do,* I wanted to illustrate the process whereby a woman is broken down by intimidation, by lies, by triangulation with her superiors, by threats about her family's welfare, and by accusations that she is acting out gender-stereotypical behaviors, such as being irrational, petty, difficult, tedious, hysterical, et cetera. I also wanted to model the behavior of a woman who refuses to be bamboozled or intimidated. Moulton's example was a steady reminder to Kelsey that she was not crazy, not imagining a conspiracy, and that she was not the one who was out-of-line.

I also wanted to illustrate the mentality behind corporate medicine, where the fiscal bottom line appears to supersede moral concerns. I wanted to show the banality of patriarchal institutions and of the men who run them. I wanted to show the unfolding horror of a decision-making process that maximizes profits at the expense of the consumers, who were being disabled by the very drugs that were supposed to heal. The title of the play, is taken from Shakespeare: "The evil that men do lives after them." It refers to the legacy of heart-breaking and life-threatening birth defects that resulted from the corporate denial and cover-up of the drug companies. This corruption played itself out along racist and misogynist lines, and the history of drugs today is still filled with examples similar to the thalidomide scandal.

Since 1960, the date of the thalidomide "scare" in this country, companies whose products are designed for women have continued to follow dangerous and deceptive practices.

Today Dr. Barbara Moulton is not widely remembered for her fight, but that fight is memorialized in the enduring recognition that her mentoree,

Dr. Francis Kelsey won for preventing the distribution of thalidomide in this country. It is important for women who are considering exposing perpetrators to remember that their example is powerful, that their voices do reverberate beyond the judges' chambers and hearing rooms where they may or may not gain credibility and where their case may or may not be won. The Francis Kelsey's of this world could not exist without the unsung heroines, like Barbara Moulton, who came before.

A Labor Play

This play was a direct response to the infamous "Baby M" case that was in the news at the time. I was very active in the Portland, Oregon, chapter of the National Organization for Women, and it had shocked me to find that one of our officers took sides with the adoptive father who was forcing the "surrogate" mother to honor her contract with him, even though she had changed her mind subsequent to the birth of her daughter. My friend felt that the issue was one of accountability: The woman had signed a legal contract as a consenting adult, and it was irresponsible for her to go back on that agreement, or to expect any sympathy from the courts. In fact, my friend contended, it was anti-feminist to argue on her behalf, because to do so would be to buy into the stereotype that women are irrational creatures, victims of our hormonal fluxes, and so on. I had a very different take on the situation, maybe because I had been separated from my mother for the first three days of my life, a traumatic estrangement that has had consequences which continue to reverberate across the landscape of my intimate relationships.

In my experience, the body has its own mandates, and we are arrogant to think that we can intellectually override these by framing them in dissociative paradigms—such as the one that equates the mother-child bond with legally transferable ownership. This is the same kind of arrogance that can manufacture artificial substances, label them "food," and then expect that there will be no biological consequences for ingesting them. This play was written in the late 1980's, but in recent literature, such as *The Primal Wound: Understanding the Adopted Child*, the truth is beginning to be told about adoption and the trauma of separation from the birth mother. However "consensual" this arrangement may be among adults, it is never with the consensus of the infant, who suffers the consequences for the rest of his or her life. And, indeed, many of these consenting birth mothers are beginning to tell their stories of unanticipated lifelong grief and depression following their ceremonial, and even celebratory, "handing over" of their babies.

In *A Labor Play*, I wanted to attack this materialist, consumerist objectification of a relationship that is, in my mind, a sacred and inviolable one in the natural world. Rather than argue against the "contract law" model, however, I decided to work within it, coming at it from a Marxist perspective: If the mother is no more than a worker hired to assemble the components for a manufactured commodity (the baby), then doesn't she have a revolutionary mandate to interrogate the social conditions and economic forces that assign her that status, and if these conditions are found to be exploitative and oppressive, isn't she justified in attempting to seize the means of distribution—that is, keep the baby?

I also wanted to make explicit the fact that this "job," like prostitution, is only considered appropriate for women in the underclasses. Nothing angers me more than middle-class intellectuals who argue for the legitimacy of prostitution and surrogacy as "work," when they would never dream of allowing their bodies to be exploited in these ways. When the boss suggests that one of the manager's daughters might want to hire herself out for the manufacture of babies, the manager responds with shock, having obviously assumed that his class background would put members of his family beyond that consideration.

In the years since I wrote the play, the brokering of babies through surrogacy and adoption, especially foreign adoption, has burgeoned beyond anything I could have imagined in 1989. Prior to the Korean War, foreign adoption may have been a private affair between individuals of conscience and desperate charities, but since the 1950's, the picture has changed radically. Foreign adoption has become an industry, one that is still largely—and horrifically—unregulated, shot through with corruption and intrigue, and with close ties to the same interests that control prostitution and trafficking in girls and women.

Critiques of surrogacy and foreign adoption are muted in the mainstream, which aligns itself with the interests of middle-class consumers. No one wants to look too deeply into the conditions and circumstances of these women who are supposedly "giving up" their children so willingly and so beneficently. And, because the infant cannot speak and the birth mothers have no voice politically, a movement of adult foreign adoptees is, at present, one of the loudest voices challenging these corporate, capitalist myths about adoption, and courageously speaking out about the profound trauma of separation from the birth mother, about the atrocity of profiteering from these separations, and the horror of normalizing the globalization of the practice.

Heterosexuals Anonymous

What if the privileging of the hetero-patriarchal perspective of the world operates as an addiction in the lives of women, warping our thoughts and causing us to obsess over and be attracted to relationships that will destroy us? What would a recovery program for this addiction look like? Would holding onto a "gynocentric" view of the world be as radical a shift in perspective as sobriety for an alcoholic? And what kind of support systems and recovery programs would women need in order to keep the focus on our feminist values and ourselves?

The P.E. Teacher

In *The P. E. Teacher,* Dana, who has credentials as an elite athlete, has accepted a job as a middle school, P.E. teacher. Her self-confidence, her feminism, and her confrontational style are out of place in this public school, where faculty members are enmeshed in a web of lies and secrets surrounding the resignation of the previous P.E. teacher. Dana's confrontation of a gay male teacher over his response to the male students' fascination with pornography alienates both him and the guidance counselor, whose job it is to smooth over such incidents. Her persistent questions about her predecessor get another teacher in trouble, and her outrage over the cover-up of harassment of female students leads to a showdown with the vice principal.

I was interested in exploring intersections of racism, misogyny, adultism, and homophobia in a public middle school, and I was also intrigued by the idea of an aggressive, lesbian athletic coach in an environment filled with mediocre bureaucrats playing petty political games. How would this woman, who is a master of game strategy and who is wired to win, survive in an environment like this—especially when the game she insists on playing is one with different stakes?

As a whistleblower in a department-wide, university credit scandal, I had a personal experience of being the target of an institutional witch-hunt, and, later, one of my artistic colleagues was scapegoated out of her teaching jobs in the public schools because of her affiliation with my lesbian theatre company. The first situation involved a million-dollar lawsuit, and the second resulted in the ACLU taking the case and promoting it as a "national priority lawsuit." Ten years after these cases, I found myself in the position of advocating for a female student who had been raped on another campus, and I found myself pitted against an administration invested in protecting their scholarship athlete/rapist. These experiences obviously inform the script, and Dana, overwhelmed by superior odds, embraces the status of an outlaw and a criminal.

The Gage and Mr. Comstock

I wrote this little one-hander in response to a call for submissions for ten-minute plays about historical figures from upstate New York. Of course, I thought immediately of my namesake, Matilda Joslyn Gage, whose home was in Fayetteville. The restoration of this home and establishment of it as an historical landmark has taken place over the last twenty years, and I have been following these developments with interest.

One of the personal anecdotes about Gage tells how she was in a kind of "post-partum" depression after the publication of her lifework *Woman, Church, and State*, but, as soon as she received word that the book had been banned by Anthony Comstock, she rose from her bed and swung into action.

I had similar experiences with debilitation during my years with my theatre company. It was the apathy of my own community, the indifference and obscurity, which were so debilitating. It became a measure of status to be taken seriously enough to have an enemy.

I also wanted to write something that would allow me to share some information with audiences about the significance of Gage's book—never more timely than in this era of rising, global fundamentalism.

Finally, I found the story of Comstock especially apt, when our current administration is hell-bent to roll back abortion rights and institute "abstinence only" teaching policies in the schools.

Black Eye

A Knockout in Nine Minutes

Black Eye

A Knockout in Nine Minutes

The year is 1953 and the setting is a middle-school principal's office and the waiting area outside the door. Amanda, a thirteen-year-old tomboy, is waiting disconsolately on a bench. She sports a brand new black eye, and has apparently been fighting.

Her P.E. teacher, Miss Marshall, has been summoned to a consultation about the incident with the principal. On the way to his office, she checks in with Amanda, and the audience understands that she has been coaching the girl on her fighting skills.

The principal, Mr. Kent, is expelling Amanda and is hoping that Miss Marshall will be willing to convey the news to both Amanda and to her mother, as Miss Marshall is the girl's favorite teacher. Miss Marshall is angered by the decision, arguing that the fight was provoked by the boys' homophobic harassment.

When Mr. Kent attempts to terminate the meeting, Miss Marshall admits that she has taught the girl how to defend herself, and she informs him that she believes in fighting. She threatens to "out" Mr. Kent to the school board if he follows through on the expulsion. Mr. Kent is confident that she will not do this, as he knows that she is also in a same-sex relationship. Miss Marshall manages to trump his ace, however, and he agrees not to expel Amanda.

Leaving the office, Miss Marshall has a final, triumphant and subversive interaction with her student.

A woman, a girl, and a man
Single set
Ten minutes

Cast of Characters

MISS MARSHALL: The P.E. teacher, a woman in her 30's.

AMANDA: The tomboy, a girl in her early teens with a bandaged knee and a black eye.

MR. KENT: The principal of a middle school, a man in his 40's.

Scene

The principal's office of a middle school.

Time

1953.

Black Eye

A middle school somewhere—anywhere—in the United States. The set is divided into two areas: the waiting area outside the principal's office, and the interior of the principal's office. The year is 1953, and, just to provide context, this is five years after the publication of Sexual Behavior in the Human Male, the first volume of The Kinsey Reports. It is the same year as the publication of the second volume: Sexual Behavior in the Human Female. A thirteen-year-old "tomgirl," in pigtails with her shirttail untucked, sits disconsolately on a bench outside the office, apparently waiting to be disciplined. She has a black eye and a bandage on her knee. Her name is AMANDA. A woman enters the waiting area from the hallway. She is tall, with short, unstyled hair, no makeup, no jewelry, and extremely sensible shoes. She does wear a skirt, because, after all, this is 1953. This is MISS MARSHALL, the physical education teacher. And, yes, she is. As she enters, AMANDA looks up.

AMANDA: Miss Marshall?

MISS MARSHALL: Hi, Mandy.

AMANDA: Are they gonna expel me?

MISS MARSHALL: I don't know. It *is* your third fight this term…

AMANDA: *(Protesting.)* But it was the boys who—

MISS MARSHALL: *(Cutting her off.)* I know… I know… But you know the school has a policy. *(AMANDA looks down. MISS MARSHALL takes pity on her.)* Let's see that fist.

AMANDA: *(Looking up.)* What?

MISS MARSHALL: The fist you used.

AMANDA: *(Brightening.)* Oh… *(She shows MISS MARSHALL her fist.)*

MISS MARSHALL: Did you remember to keep your thumb tucked?

AMANDA: *(Eager to please her mentor.)* I did!

MISS MARSHALL: And you threw your punch from the shoulder, not the elbow?

AMANDA: *(Becoming very excited.)* Yes, ma'am! You wanna see it? *(MISS MARSHALL smiles. AMANDA rises.)* Well, Roy was standin' here, and Tommy's here, and Sam is behind him, so I figure if I punch Tommy first, he's gonna fall into Sam, which is gonna give me enough time to take care of Roy. SO… I turned kinda sideways to Tommy, so's to keep an eye on Roy, like this—*(Just then the door to the principal's office opens, and MR. KENT appears standing in the doorway. MR. KENT is the principal. He is impeccably dressed with a striped tie that matches the grey of his suit as well as the blue of his eyes. His wavy, blond hair would make him appear younger than his forty years, were it not offset by a pair of severe wire-rimmed glasses. He is, as they say, "light in the loafers." MR. KENT clears his throat, and AMANDA freezes.)*

AMANDA: Mr. Kent!

MR. KENT: *(Sternly, but not unkindly.)* Amanda. *(He turns to the P.E. teacher.)* Miss Marshall, I appreciate your coming by the office on such short notice.

MISS MARSHALL: Not at all. You caught me between my sixth grade P.E. class and my fifth-grade health class.

MR. KENT: *(To AMANDA.)* Now, young lady, if you don't mind waiting a few more minutes, I would like to speak to Miss Marshall first. *(AMANDA drops anxiously back on her bench. MR. KENT waits to usher MISS MARSHALL into his office. She follows him, but, just before reaching the door, she turns with her back to the principal, smiles at AMANDA, and holds up both her fists. AMANDA bursts into a huge grin, and just as she is holding up her fists in salute, MR.KENT turns and catches the gesture. She quickly pretends to be grooming her pigtails, a look of contrition on her face. The two adults disappear into the office, and as the door closes, AMANDA jumps up, performing a victory dance, which includes a replay of the knockout punches. The lights go out on the waiting area and come up in the principal's office.)*

MR. KENT: Well, Miss Marshall, I think we have ourselves a situation. *(He laughs, and MISS MARSHALL smiles.)* I understand she knocked one of the boys unconscious.

MISS MARSHALL: Roy Dobbins.

MR. KENT: Roy! *(MR. KENT nods and laughs again.)*

MISS MARSHALL: And she knocked out Tommy Crawford's front teeth. *(He shakes his head.)* Poor Sam got the worst of it. *Two* black eyes and a broken nose.

MR. KENT: *(Wiping his glasses.)* Well, I'm sure they had it coming.

MISS MARSHALL: They did. They harass all the girls, but especially Amanda... *Her eyes meet his.)*... Because she's different.

MR. KENT: *(Uncomfortable.)* I don't doubt it. Well... take a look at this and tell me what you think. *(He hands her a piece of paper.)*

MISS MARSHALL: What is it?

MR. KENT: It's the letter of expulsion to Amanda's mother.

MISS MARSHALL: *(Reading it and handing it back.)* What do you want me to say?

MR. KENT: Well, I know you're Amanda's favorite teacher, and that you've met with her mother, so I was hoping that you might be able to help her understand—

MISS MARSHALL: *(Cutting him off.)* I don't understand. The boys started it. Amanda was only defending herself.

MR. KENT: Miss Marshall, the boys were using *words.* I can't expel them for that. Amanda chose to use her fists.

MISS MARSHALL: Sometimes that's what it takes to be heard. And words can cut deeper than a knife. You must know that. *(An uncomfortable pause.)*

MR. KENT: Well, the school has a policy—

MISS MARSHALL: *(Cutting him off.)* Maybe it needs a new policy.

MR. KENT: Maybe that's true, and that's certainly something you can propose to the school board the next time it meets.

MISS MARSHALL: Which will be too late for Amanda.

MR. KENT: She made a strong choice, Miss Marshall. And she has caused some serious injuries… *(MISS MARSHALL says nothing. MR. KENT drums on his desk for a moment. Looking up, he becomes very formal.)* I'm sorry… I was hoping that you might be willing to make this easier for the girl, but I can see that you're uncomfortable with that, and I accept that. So, thank you—*(He rises to usher her out of the office.)*

MISS MARSHALL: Mr. Kent—

MR. KENT: *(Turning.)* Yes?

MISS MARSHALL: I would like to ask you a question. May I?

MR. KENT: *(Uneasy.)* I suppose.

MISS MARSHALL: Did you fight?

MR. KENT: What?

MISS MARSHALL: Did you fight?

MR. KENT: *(Confused.)* They wouldn't take me… My eyesight was poor—

MISS MARSHALL: I didn't mean the War. I meant did you fight when they called you names? When you were Amanda's age?

MR. KENT: I'm not sure what you're getting at, Miss Marshall.

MISS MARSHALL: I think you know exactly what I'm getting at, Mr. Kent. And I want to know, "Did you fight back?"

MR. KENT: *(After a long silence.)* No, I did not. All they had to do was take my glasses, and I was at their mercy.

MISS MARSHALL: So what did you do… if I may ask?

MR. KENT: *(A very long pause.)* Actually, I became skillful at negotiating. I would find out what I had that might be useful to certain of them—composing their papers for them, or buying them things. And I would create alliances.

MISS MARSHALL: *(Nodding.)* Well, Amanda is not a good student, and her family is poor. But she can fight and she can win.

MR. KENT: Outside of school, Miss Marshall… outside of school. *(He opens the door. MISS MARSHALL closes it, again.)*

MISS MARSHALL: I taught her.

MR. KENT: *(Taken aback.)* What?

MISS MARSHALL: I taught her to fight. She wanted to learn.

MR. KENT: I see. Do you want me to have to fire you as well?

MISS MARSHALL: Not at all. I want you to understand that I believe in fighting. And I will fight you.

MR. KENT: I see. And just how do you propose to do that?

MISS MARSHALL: I shall send an anonymous letter to the school board suggesting that your morals might be somewhat less than what is desirable in a school principal and that they might want to look into your living situation with your "housemate."

MR. KENT: *(Smiling.)* You hardly seem in the position to make that threat. There have already been more than a few rumors about the P.E. teacher and her "companion."

MISS MARSHALL: Teachers lose their jobs all the time, Mr. Kent, and for a variety of reasons, but it's more unusual for a school administrator— especially a principal— to resign suddenly in the middle of the term, and especially after so many years of outstanding service.

MR. KENT: *(A long pause.)* And just how would you propose explaining to these boys' parents and to the school board why this girl is still here?

MISS MARSHALL: You're a clever man. This could be a real opportunity to exercise those skills at negotiation and alliances.

MR. KENT: Touché. And now, may I ask you a question? *(She smiles.)* Why do you care so much about this girl?

MISS MARSHALL: *(Angry at the insinuation and dead serious.)* Because that's my job.

MR. KENT: *(He looks at her for a moment, and then, with a sigh, he drops the letter of expulsion into the trash.)* You win.

MISS MARSHALL: Thank you, Mr. Kent. It's been a pleasure. *(She exits. As she leaves, the lights come up on the waiting area. AMANDA leaps up, anxious to hear the verdict. MISS MARSHALL looks at her sternly for a moment, before she speaks.)* Report to class early tomorrow and I'll teach you the roundhouse kick. *(MISS MARSHALL begins to exit, and we hear MR. KENT calling from his office:)*

MR. KENT: *(Offstage.)* Amanda…!

AMANDA: Yes, sir! *(She runs to his door, turns, and looks back at her teacher. MISS MARSHALL holds up her fists, and AMANDA returns the gesture.)*

Blackout

End of Play

The Ladies' Room

A Play in Five Minutes

The Ladies' Room

A Play in Five Minutes

The play opens in a ladies' room at a shopping mall. A woman has just gone to report to the security guard that there is a man in the bathroom. The "man" is actually Rae, a teenage, lesbian butch. Angry and humiliated in front of her partner, Rae is hurling taunts and insults after the woman.

Her girlfriend Nicole is uncomfortable about the dynamic, and the two begin to argue.

When Nicole expresses concern that public bathrooms are a common site for assault, Rae ridicules her for buying into an urban myth. As Nicole defends herself, it becomes apparent that she has been a victim of a stranger rape in a public space.

Rae is emotionally overwhelmed by this information. At this point, her accuser is seen returning with the security guard, and Rae must decide how to respond.

Two teenaged girls, one with masculine gender presentation
Single set
6 minutes

Cast of Characters

RAE: A lesbian butch, 17.

NICOLE: Her partner, 17.

Scene

Outside a ladies' room in a shopping mall.

Time

The present.

The Ladies' Room

The scene takes place outside the door of a ladies' room at a shopping mall. The door has the silhouette of a figure in a dress to signify that it is a women's bathroom. The present.

There has just been an ugly confrontation, in which a woman using the restroom has accused RAE of being a man. RAE is a seventeen-year-old, lesbian butch with masculine gender presentation. This kind of confrontation happens to her frequently. She is with her teenage girlfriend, NICOLE, who has never been mistaken for a man. As young, working-class lesbians, both of these women are constant targets for homophobic violence and/or sexual harassment. They love each other deeply, and this love is invisible or derided by the culture.

The woman who confronted RAE has gone to report her to the mall security guard. RAE, insulted and humiliated, is yelling after her. Nicole is upset by the confrontation, and also by her partner's verbal aggression.

RAE: *(Yelling.)* Yeah! You call the mall security guard! You do that! Why don't you call the fucking gender police while you're at it?

NICOLE: *(Upset.)* Rae…

RAE: *(Still yelling.)* What are you going to do? Arrest me? Arrest me for trying to use a fucking bathroom in a shopping mall? Yeah! You do that! You arrest me! *(Turning back.)* Asshole.

NICOLE: Okay, Rae…

RAE: What do you mean, "Okay, Rae?" You heard her…! "There's a man in the ladies' room! There's a man in the ladies' room!" Oh, no! The sky is falling!

NICOLE: Okay…

RAE: No! *Not* "okay!" I have to go through this fucking bullshit every day… every time I have to use a public bathroom!

NICOLE: I know. I'm sorry.

RAE: Yeah, well, I didn't hear *you* saying anything…

14

NICOLE: I didn't know what to say.

RAE: Yeah, well *I* do. *(Yelling after the woman.)* Fuck you!

NICOLE: That's not going to help.

RAE: *(Overwhelmed with rage and frustration.) Nothing's* going to help! That's the world I live in, and it's *fucked!*

NICOLE: It's a public restroom, Rae—

RAE: Exactly! *Public!* So where does she get off deciding who gets to use it? *(Yelling again.)* Is there a *dress code?*

NICOLE: She thought you were a man.

RAE: And what if I was? It's none of her fucking business. What if I was transitioning? *(NICOLE turns away, unable to deal with her partner's rage.)* What? Don't tell me you think it is!

NICOLE: *(Weary.)* Is what?

RAE: Her business… how I dress …?

NICOLE: No…

RAE: No… but what?

NICOLE: *(Looking away.)* It's a public bathroom. Men rape women in public bathrooms.

RAE: *(Exploding.)* Oh, that is just *bullshit*! Paranoid bullshit they always pull out to reinforce their stupid gender codes!

NICOLE: No, it isn't.

RAE: Oh, come on, Nicole! Whose side are you on?

NICOLE: It's not about sides.

RAE: Look, some woman I never saw in my life, right now, is reporting me to some stupid mall security guard as we speak, just for trying to take a piss in a freakin' public bathroom. You're either on her side or you're on my side!

15

NICOLE: It's not about you.

RAE: Well, it's sure as hell not about you!

NICOLE: Actually, it is.

RAE: What? You think she's reporting you?

NICOLE: No.

RAE: Then how is it about you?

NICOLE: I already told you, but you didn't want to hear it.

RAE: What?

NICOLE: You don't even remember.

RAE: What? Oh, that "men rape women in public bathrooms?" *(NICOLE is silent.)* Is that it? *(Silence.)* Come on… Is that it?

NICOLE: Yeah. That's it. *(There is a long silence. RAE shakes her head.)*

RAE: I can't believe you buy into that urban-myth shit.

NICOLE: It's not an urban myth. Bathrooms are the third most common sites of stranger rape.

RAE: Yeah? And what are the first two?

NICOLE: Grocery store parking lots and office parking garages.

RAE: Yeah, right. So women are supposed to be afraid to eat and go to work. *(NICOLE looks at her.)* Oh, yeah… and pee.

NICOLE: You don't get it.

RAE: I *do* get it. *You're* the one not getting it, Nicole! It's about controlling women. It's the same as the gender-police thing.

NICOLE: No, it's not! You're talking about how you *dress*, how you *look*. This is about *rapists*! We can't help it if they stalk us.

RAE: *(Facetious.)* Well, we could just quit going anywhere or doing anything where anyone could ever even *think* about attacking us... like maybe just stay in the house all the time—

NICOLE: *(Enraged, NICOLE cuts her off.)* And I've done that! *(RAE is shocked. NICOLE looks down.)* And that doesn't work either. *(There is a long silence.)*

RAE: Shit... I'm sorry...

NICOLE: *(Escalating.)* And you know something? I *like* it when women protect each other! I *like* it that a woman who thinks there is a man in the bathroom goes and reports it to the security guard! Even when she gets yelled at and insulted for doing it... I *like* that! I *like* when a woman waits to see if another woman gets into her car in a parking garage before she drives off. I *like* that!

RAE: *(Very quiet.)* I didn't know ...

NICOLE: *(Cutting her off.)* That's because I didn't tell you. *(A long silence.)*

RAE: Was it in a bathroom?

NICOLE: No.   *(After another long silence, NICOLE lets out a sigh.)* A parking deck... stairwell.

RAE: I'm sorry... Nicole?

NICOLE: *(Her anger dissipating.)* So am I. And I'm sorry that woman talked to you like that. And I'm sorry I didn't say anything, because I couldn't think of anything to say. And I'm sorry we're fighting. Let's go.

RAE: *(Looking at her.)* I love you so much. *(Weary, NICOLE puts her arms around RAE. Suddenly RAE starts to cry.)*

NICOLE: It was before I met you.

RAE: *(Crying.)* I'm so sorry... God, Nicole...

NICOLE: *(Detaching.)* Here they come... Let's go.

RAE: *(Turning her back to wipe her eyes.)* Shit.

NICOLE: Come on, Rae...

RAE: *(Still turned.)* No, wait.

NICOLE: They're *coming. (She is pulling on RAE, but suddenly RAE turns to face her accusers.)*

NICOLE: Rae—! What are you doing?

RAE: I'm going to show them my ID. *(NICOLE is shocked.)*

NICOLE: Really?

RAE: *(Bracing.)* Yeah. I'm going to show them my ID. *(Taking out her wallet.)* You go on. *(NICOLE hesitates for a minute and then takes RAE's hand, standing shoulder-to-shoulder as they wait for the security guard.)*

Blackout

End of Play

The A-Mazing Yamashita and the Millennial Gold-Diggers

The Transnational Magic Show of the Millennium

This play is dedicated to the truly A-Mazing Mary Daly
and her alchemical writings.

The A-Mazing Yamashita and The Millennial Gold Diggers

The Transnational Magic Show of the Millennium

Yamashita is a female magician, who promises us an evening of entertainment, where she will personally escort her audience "through the secret tunnels and nubiferous passageways of a post-colonialist, global economic maze, more hidden than King Solomon's Tomb, more baffling than the riddle of the Sphinx and more impenetrable than the Great Pyramid of Khufu."

In fact, her Assistant has run away, and the A-Mazing Yamashita is compelled to recruit volunteers from the audience for her classic acts of levitating a woman, sawing a woman in half, and causing a woman to vanish in a magic cabinet, the Cabinet of GATT (yes, as in "General Agreements on Tariff and Trade").

In the course of her highly unorthodox magic, the Assistant returns via the Cabinet, to warn the audience that Yamashita is actually trafficking the women who volunteer for her magic acts. Yamashita, assuring the audience that this is all part of the act, produces a young Thai woman who has "chosen" to prostitute herself, illustrating the "magic" of GATT in generating market conditions that disappear women. Entering the Cabinet herself, Yamashita manages to convince the Stage Manager that there is no need for intervention.

When her Assistant takes matters into her own hands, telephoning the police, Yamashita must disappear her volunteers as well as her Assistant. To allay our fears about the reality of what we are seeing, she calls in a women's studies professor, who uses post-structuralist theory to deconstruct audience questions. Finally, Yamashita undertakes the mass hypnosis of her entire audience. Explaining how the synaptic association of inequality with sexual arousal will eliminate any sense of discomfort about the evening, and, in fact, greatly enhance the audience's ability to participate in the new global economy, Yamashita proceeds with a slideshow of pornographic imagery. At this point, the Stage Manager pulls the electrical plug and the fate of the evening lies in the hands of the audience.

Seven women
One man
Two teenaged girls, one Asian
Three adults, any gender

Cast of Characters

THE A-MAZING YAMASHITA: A female magician, any age.

STAGE MANAGER: A lesbian butch, any age.

FIRST VOLUNTEER: A woman, any age.

FIRST VOLUNTEER'S BOYFRIEND: A man, any age.

SECOND VOLUNTEER: A woman, any age.

THIRD VOLUNTEER: A large woman, any age.

FOURTH VOLUNTEER: A woman with a traditionally "sexy" figure.

ASSISTANT: An African American, teenaged girl.

THAI GIRL: An Asian, teenaged girl.

PROFESSOR YESSIR: A middle-aged, middle-class, white woman.

WOMAN: A woman, any age.

EMERGENCY MEDICAL TECHNICIAN: A man or woman.

POLICE OFFICER: A man, any age.

HOUSE MANAGER: A man or woman.

Scene
A cabaret theatre space.

Time
The present.

The A-Mazing Yamashita and the Millennial Gold Diggers

A cabaret stage with the magician's props, boxes, and other contraptions littered about. Downstage left is the Great Cabinet of GATT. Curtain rises on a dark stage. There is a sudden explosion and flash of light. The A-MAZING YAMASHITA, a professional magician, emerges from the smoke. She stands center stage in a spotlight. YAMASHITA's speech is very rapid and accompanied by gestures that are intended to confuse and distract. If the role is played by an actual magician, it would be appropriate to embellish her speeches with sleight-of-hand tricks.

YAMASHITA: Good evening, ladies and gentlemen. Welcome to Yamashita's Labyrinth of Lost Treasures and Stolen Pleasures, where, for the next hour, you will be regaled with acts of magic and feats of mystery that will amaze, astound, and confound you, as the A-Mazing Yamashita— *(She bows. The following speech is punctuated with drum rolls.)*… will personally escort you through the secret tunnels and nubiferous passageways of a post-colonialist, post-structuralist, global economic maze, more hidden than King Solomon's Tomb, more baffling than the riddle of the Sphinx and more impenetrable than the Great Pyramid of Khufu—Tonight, before your very eyes, you will witness the laws of gravity—and *gravitas*!—displaced by the levitational puissance of selective serotonin reuptake inhibitors... you will gasp in wonder at the partition of a human female —a bi-sectional, post-modern deconstruction that will enable her to function more… "liberally" than prior to her dorsal disassociation... Finally, you will be initiated into the intricate mysteries of the Great Cabinet of GATT, where, ladies and gentlemen, you will witness the disappearing of not just one woman, not just a dozen women, not even a hundred women...! Ladies and gentlemen, tonight for your entertainment, edification—and not inconsiderable financial advantage!—you will witness the dematerialization of *one hundred and thirteen million women*… And now for my first trick... *My hat, please! (Drum roll. She extends her arm. Nothing happens.)* My hat, please! *(Drum roll. She extends her arm again. She pauses for a moment and then crosses to the wings.)* You...! You... Stage Manager! *(The STAGE MANAGER enters.)* Where is my assistant?

STAGE MANAGER: I don't know.

YAMASHITA: Isn't she backstage?

STAGE MANAGER: Haven't seen her. *(YAMASHITA pauses and then notices the lock on the Cabinet of GATT. She crosses accusingly to the STAGE MANAGER.)*

YAMASHITA: Someone has been tampering with the lock on the Great Cabinet of GATT!

STAGE MANAGER: Nobody's been backstage except your assistant.

YAMASHITA: Exactly.

STAGE MANAGER: Well, don't look at me... She's *your* assistant!

YAMASHITA: I thought it was your job to guard the props and not let anyone touch them!

STAGE MANAGER: It's not *my* job to supervise *your* assistant.

YAMASHITA: Did you see where she went?

STAGE MANAGER: Maybe she's in the cabinet. *(YAMASHITA considers for a moment, and then produces a key, crosses swiftly to the Cabinet, and locks it.)* Wait! What if she's in there...?

YAMASHITA: *(Winking.)* Don't worry! This is just part of the show! Thank you... And now if you could just get me my hat...? *(The STAGE MANAGER exits and YAMASHITA turns to the audience.)* Well, it seems that my assistant has done a little vanishing act of her own. Never mind. I don't need her. I'm sure we can manage just fine with a volunteer from the audience... But first... *(Calling to the wings.)* My hat... *(A pause.)* My *hat!* *(A top hat comes sailing from the wings. YAMASHITA, enraged, pauses for a moment before picking it up.)* Ladies and gentlemen... just a hat... *(YAMASHITA shows the audience the inside of it of the hat, Putting it on her head, she crosses to the FIRST VOLUNTEER and her BOYFRIEND seated in the front row.)* You! *(The FIRST VOLUNTEER cringes.)* Yes, you! Do you want to levitate? *(The FIRST VOLUNTEER shakes her head.)* No...? You *don't* want to levitate? *(Silence.)* You don't think it would be pleasant to experience yourself rising above the cares and worries that chain us all to this mortal coil? *(The FIRST VOLUNTEER shakes her head again. The following exchange is very rapid, almost like an auctioneer's patter.)* Oh, come on. It's easy. *(The FIRST VOLUNTEER shakes her head again. YAMASHITA pulls a bill out of her hat.)* Twenty dollars...? Thirty...? *(The FIRST VOLUNTEER shakes her head. YAMASHITA sighs. She begins to count out bills.)* One hundred dollars? *(The BOYFRIEND whispers something to the FIRST VOLUNTEER. She still shakes her head.)* Ladies and gentlemen, she has turned down the hundred dollars! *To the BOYFRIEND.)* Are you the boyfriend? *(He nods.)* Your girlfriend has just turned down one hundred dollars to help me out. What do you think of that? *(He does not respond.)* How about five hundred dollars! Five hundred dollars if your girlfriend volunteers! *(He looks at the FIRST VOLUNTEER. She nods to him. YAMASHITA turns to her.)* You'll do it? *(The FIRST VOLUNTEER nods.)* You'll do it if I give him five hundred dollars? *(The FIRST VOLUNTEER nods again.)* Ladies, and gentlemen—five hundred dollars for her first trick! *(To the woman.)* Not bad. Now—*(She counts out the bills to the BOYFRIEND.)*... if you'll just step up here... *(As the FIRST VOLUNTEER mounts the stage, YAMASHITA wheels in a platform.)* I need you to lie down on the Imperial Palanquin of the Odalisque. *(FIRST VOLUNTEER hesitates.)* You do know what an odalisque is, don't you...? *(To the audience.)* A female slave in charge of other women in the harem. *(To FIRST VOLUNTEER.)* Can you say it...? "Odalisque."

FIRST VOLUNTEER: Odalisque.

YAMASHITA: Let's all say it... "Odalisque" *(She waits for the audience response, and then turns back to the VOLUNTEER.)* Now, lie down... *(FIRST VOLUNTEER whispers something to YAMASHITA.)* She wants to know what's going to happen to her! Five hundred dollars for ten minutes of work, and she still wants a job description! *(YAMASHITA laughs. The FIRST VOLUNTEER lies down.)* Ladies and gentlemen, please. I need your absolute concentration for this. We are going to levitate this woman. *(To FIRST VOLUNTEER.)* But don't worry... it's very safe. Listen to me! You will feel yourself rising, floating... up, up, up... higher and higher until you can look down on all your problems and all your cares, and they will seem so tiny, like little specks, because you are *so* high... Now, close your eyes... *(FIRST VOLUNTEER closes her eyes.)*... and think of clouds. *(Pause.)* Are you thinking of clouds? *(FIRST VOLUNTEER nods.)* Not thunderclouds... White, fluffy, puffy clouds... are you thinking of them? *(FIRST VOLUNTEER nods. Pause. YAMASHITA turns to the audience.)* All of you—think of clouds—*Now!* *(Pause. To the audience.)* Are you all thinking of clouds? *(Pause. YAMASHITA appears puzzled.)* I don't understand. She's still not levitating... There must be something wrong... Something I've overlooked... Wait! I know! She is depressed! *(To FIRST VOLUNTEER.)* Aren't you? You have taken five hundred dollars of my money to levitate, and you did not tell me that you were depressed.

FIRST VOLUNTEER: I didn't know I was...

YAMASHITA: Ah! And you're thinking of clouds, aren't you?

FIRST VOLUNTEER: Yes!

YAMASHITA: But you're not levitating, are you?

FIRST VOLUNTEER: No...

YAMASHITA: Do you think we are depressing you?

FIRST VOLUNTEER: No...

YAMASHITA: *(Conclusively.)* Well! What are we going to do? I've given your boyfriend five hundred dollars of my money—Yamashita's own money!—for you to levitate... but, I'll tell you what—I'm going to let your boyfriend keep the money, because you are going to take a little pill for this depression. A little anti-gravity pill. *(She materializes a bottle of anti-depressants.)*

FIRST VOLUNTEER: *(Reading the label.)* Don't you need a prescription for those?

YAMASHITA: Ladies and gentlemen — you see with your own eyes that this woman will not, cannot levitate. And right now, as you sit here, forty-three million women are taking these pills. One out of every ten women in this country is taking these pills. One out of three women who are sitting in doctors' offices this very minute are there specifically to collect these little pills. Four billion dollars they are paying... *four billion dollars*! *(To the FIRST VOLUNTEER.)* Did you know that there are so many people taking anti-depressants in the U.K., it's turning up in our municipal water supply? *We're all taking them! (Throwing back her head and laughing, she turns to the BOYFRIEND.)* But your girlfriend says she needs a prescription. *(She holds out her hand to the BOYFRIEND for the money. He starts to hand it back.)*

FIRST VOLUNTEER: I just don't think I'm depressed...

YAMASHITA: So, you think there is something wrong with my magic? There's no money in that, is there? *(To audience.)* And no show. So what, ladies and gentlemen, should she do? AND if there is no money and no show, then we'll all have to take a little pill, won't we? Because what is life without the money or the show? *(Turning viciously to the VOLUNTEER.)* Do you want us all to be depressed, just because you don't think you are? *(FIRST VOLUNTEER is confused. YAMASHITA laughs.)* I am joking with you. *(To the audience.)* I tell you what. We'll play a little game. *(To the VOLUNTEER.)* Now, here is the pill... *(To the audience.)*

25

And you're going to help her with this. *(To the VOLUNTEER.)* They're going to help you. *(To the audience and the VOLUNTEER.)* Now, watch my hands. *(She makes several passes.)* Now... Which hand has the pill? Guess correctly, and you get to take it. Guess incorrectly, and... well, no money, no show. *(To the audience.)* Which hand? *(To the audience.)* You can help her. You've paid for the show. *(The audience shouts their responses.)*

FIRST VOLUNTEER: *That* hand.

YAMASHITA: *(Opening her hand.)* Empty... but not for long! *(She crosses to the BOYFRIEND and holds out her hand for the money.)*

FIRST VOLUNTEER: No, wait! Let me try again!

YAMASHITA: You want to try again...? The A-Mazing Yamashita never repeats a trick. But, I tell you what... I will give you another chance... I will let your boyfriend keep his money—*if* you can find another volunteer who will take the pill! *(The VOLUNTEER turns toward the audience. Suddenly a woman stands up.)* A volunteer! Ladies and gentlemen, a volunteer...! *(She dismisses the FIRST VOLUNTEER. The SECOND VOLUNTEER mounts the stage. The FIRST VOLUNTEER returns to her seat.)* And what is your name, please?

SECOND VOLUNTEER: Janet.

YAMASHITA: Janet, do you have a prejudice against anti-depressants? *(The SECOND VOLUNTEER smiles conspiratorially and opens her purse. Triumphantly, she produces a prescription bottle. YAMASHITA nods and turns to the audience.)* And how much money shall we pay her for the trick?

SECOND VOLUNTEER: Oh, you don't have to pay me.

YAMASHITA: We don't? This woman's boyfriend just got $500 for his girlfriend *not* doing the trick, and you don't' want to get paid *anything*...?

SECOND VOLUNTEER: No.

YAMASHITA: *(To the audience.)* Ladies and gentlemen, this is incredible!

SECOND VOLUNTEER: I don't care about money.

YAMASHITA: You don't care about money? *(SECOND VOLUNTEER nods.)* Then, why don't you pay me? *(SECOND VOLUNTEER laughs. YAMASHITA turns to the audience.)* She thinks I'm kidding. *(To SECOND VOLUNTEER.)* So you're not doing this for the money. You're doing it for a woman you never met before, so her boyfriend can keep the money?

SECOND VOLUNTEER: Yes.

YAMASHITA: I tell you what... I'm going to hypnotize you and make you care about money. Would you like that? *(She shakes her head.)* You don't *want* to care about money? *(She shakes her head.)* Ladies and gentlemen, the woman who does not care about money! *(More applause.)* But now, I need you to lie down on the Palanquin of Odalisque...

SECOND VOLUNTEER: What about the anti-depressant?

YAMASHITA: You can't be depressed—you don't care about money! *(To the audience.)* You are thinking, "Yamashita does not know what she is talking about here." You're thinking that there are plenty of depressed people who don't care about money. Yes—you see, I can read minds, too. You didn't know that about me, did you? You see, I just did it again. *(To SECOND VOLUNTEER.)* Now, I need you to get yourself comfortable... You can leave your shoes on. *(VOLUNTEER lies down. Suddenly, there is terrible racket from the cabinet.)* And now you are thinking "Someone must be in the cabinet...?" You see, I know what you're thinking. *(To VOLUNTEER.)* Now, are you comfortable? *(More noise from the cabinet. YAMASHITA addresses the audience.)* There is no one in the Cabinet. *(Back to the VOLUNTEER, who is sitting up again.)* Good. Lie down. *(Huge racket. She turns to the audience.)* Why are you determined not to believe me? What do I need to do to prove to you that there is no one in that Cabinet?

AUDIENCE MEMBER: Open it!

YAMASHITA: Open it? You want me to open the Great Cabinet of GATT?

AUDIENCE: Yes.

YAMASHITA: *(To VOLUNTEER.)* You don't think you can ignore the noise?

SECOND VOLUNTEER: No.

YAMASHITA: All right... All right. *(Crossing to the Cabinet, she unlocks it and throws open the door.)* It's empty. *(She walks into it.)* You see?—No one there. *(She pushes open the back panel and walks through it.)* Free trade... Import, export... Give and take. In the back, out the front. In the front, out the back... *(She slams the door shut and returns to the palanquin. The Cabinet is left unlocked.)* And now, are you ready to levitate?

SECOND VOLUNTEER: Yes.

YAMASHITA: But you're not sleepy are you? How do you expect me to levitate you if you aren't sleepy? Shall I tell you a bedtime story? *(To the audience.)* We all need to tell ourselves bedtime stories, don't we...? Well... Once upon a time there was a country that invaded other countries, raiding them, raping and pillaging, and taking their money. Taking their gold. Taking their precious gold. And there was a general named Yamashita... and there are no coincidences... and General Yamashita was put in charge of all this gold, because if anyone knew about it, they might try to steal it for themselves or force him to give it back. So he decided to hide it, but it was a great big pile of gold—so what do you think he did with it? General Yamashita buried it under a mountain! This clever general had all his soldiers digging out tunnels in the side of a mountain, and then, when all of the gold was safely stored away, he blew up the entrance to the tunnel, trapping and killing all the soldiers inside. That way no one except him would ever know where he hid the gold. *(To the SECOND VOLUNTEER.)* Do you know the moral of this story? The moral of the story is, it's not enough to steal. It's not enough to hide what you've stolen. You must hide the hiders with the hidden. You must bury the buriers with the buried. *(She pauses, annoyed at their obtuseness.)* You have to collapse the tunnels of memory, no? *(Another pause.)* You will forget that I just said that! Hey presto! *(To the audience.)* Now, what is the moral of the story? What story? *(She throws back her head and laughs. Suddenly, she turns to the SECOND VOLUNTEER.)* But you haven't taken your pill yet, have you?

SECOND VOLUNTEER: But you didn't think I was depressed...

YAMASHITA: But you are depressing. You are depressing because you are not levitating, and that is the thing that *they* have paid you to do, and that *I* am being paid to do. Now, why is it that you will take a pill if you are *depressed* but you will not take one if you are depressing other people? Can you answer that for me?

SECOND VOLUNTEER: I hadn't thought about it...

YAMASHITA: Think about it! Think about it and take a pill! Take a whole bottle!

SECOND VOLUNTEER: You're kidding.

YAMASHITA: Am I? You take one pill when *you* are feeling bad about your life, yes? So how many should you take when an *entire roomful* of people are feeling bad about your life? Do the math!

SECOND VOLUNTEER: But a whole bottle would be an overdose.

YAMASHITA: Under ordinary circumstances, but these are not ordinary circumstances, are they? Don't you trust me? *(Aside to the audience.)* She *will* say yes. *(Earnestly, to the SECOND VOLUNTEER.)* Listen to me, Janet... This is part of the show. I need you to say "yes." *(Prompting her.)* "Yes...?"

SECOND VOLUNTEER: *(Thoroughly confused.)* Yes...

YAMASHITA: Then you will take the bottle. Not because I tell you to. Not because they want you to. You will take it because you have said yes... yes? *(Pause.)* I said, "Yes?"

SECOND VOLUNTEER: *(Rattled.)* Yes.

YAMASHITA: But now we will give you a little privacy. So you can concentrate. It takes concentration to levitate.

SECOND VOLUNTEER: But...

YAMASHTA: *(Annoyed.)* What? Nobody wants to watch you swallow a whole bottle of pills! It's not part of the show... *(She pulls the curtains closed again.)* And now, ladies and gentlemen, while Janet prepares herself for levitation, I shall perform a feat of magic specifically *tailored* for your enjoyment and edification. I shall partition a woman, disconnecting the upper half of her body from the lower half, and I shall perform this feat with such amazing dexterity, she will not even be aware that the operation has taken place! You do not believe me? Who will volunteer? *(The THIRD VOLUNTEER, a large or older woman, rises.)*

THIRD VOLUNTEER: I do.

YAMASHITA: *(Intentionally ignoring her, YAMASHITA turns to a young woman, who with a traditionally "sexy" figure.)* How about you? *(The FOURTH VOLUNTEER does not respond.)* One hundred dollars? No?

THIRD VOLUNTEER: Hey! I said I'd do it!

YAMASHITA: *(Ignoring her, YAMASHITA continues to speak to the FOURTH VOLUNTEER.)* Three hundred?

THIRD VOLUNTEER: Hey, what is this? *(To the audience.)* She must be a plant!

YAMASHITA: *(Still ignoring the THIRD VOLUNTEER.)* Four hundred...? Five hundred?

FOURTH VOLUNTEER: All right. *(The FOURTH VOLUNTEER rises and begins to cross to the stage.)*

THIRD VOLUNTEER: No! No, this is bullshit... I volunteered! I volunteered first! *(A HOUSE MANAGER approaches the THIRD VOLUNTEER. While they are arguing YAMASHITA is busy counting out the bills to the FOURTH VOLUNTEER.)*

HOUSE MANAGER: You have to be quiet!

THIRD VOLUNTEER: No! She called for a volunteer! I volunteered...!

HOUSE MANAGER: You have to be quiet.

THIRD VOLUNTEER: But that girl didn't even volunteer!

HOUSE MANAGER: You're going to have to leave.

THIRD VOLUNTEER: This is bullshit!

HOUSE MANAGER: Be quiet or leave! *(The THIRD VOLUNTEER sits, and the HOUSE MANAGER returns to her place.).*

YAMASHITA: *(Finishing handing over the money.)* There... And your name?

FOURTH VOLUNTEER: Stephanie.

YAMASHITA: Stephanie, have you ever been cut in two before?

FOURTH VOLUNTEER: *(Giggling.)* I don't think so.

YAMASHITA: You don't think so? Don't you think you'd remember?

FOURTH VOLUNTEER: *(Giggling.)* I guess so.

YAMASHITA: Well, Stephanie Guess-So... I have a little something for you... *(Suddenly YAMASHITA produces a box and thrusts it into the hands of the FOURTH VOLUNTEER.)* Here—

FOURTH VOLUNTEER: What is this?

YAMASHITA: Open it up and see! *(As the FOURTH VOLUNTEER removes the items, YAMASHITA names them.)* A bustier... *(Drum roll.)*... a garter... *(Drum roll.)*... fishnet stockings... *(Drum roll.)*... and... stiletto heels! *(Cymbals.)*

THIRD VOLUNTEER: *(Rising angrily.)* Oh, yeah...! That's what this is about! She wanted somebody sexy! This is bullshit! *(The HOUSE MANAGER starts to cross to her.)* You know what? This is fuckin' bullshit! *(THIRD VOLUNTEER exits the house before the HOUSE MANAGER gets to her.)*

YAMASHITA: Well... Stephanie, what do you have to say?

FOURTH VOLUNTEER: *(Nervous.)* You want me to wear those?

YAMASHITA: You don't like them?

FOURTH VOLUNTEER: *(Giggling.)* Well, no... It's just...

YAMASHITA: We are going to cut you in half, you know. Wouldn't you rather be wearing our clothes than yours... in case there's a little accident...?

FOURTH VOLUNTEER: *(Frightened.)* An accident...?

YAMASHITA: *(All business.)* The A-Mazing Yamashita is making a little joke. We need you to put on the clothes in order to perform the trick. There is a dressing room backstage. *(She steers her toward the wings. The VOLUNTEER takes the costume and exits. YAMASHITA turns to the audience.)* Now, while she is changing... and she will be changing, because they all do... I'm going to show you another trick—*(She begins to remove her hat, when suddenly, her ASSISTANT, an African American teenaged girl, bursts out of the Cabinet, collapsing on the stage. She's out-of-breath and disoriented. YAMASHITA watches her for a moment before speaking.)* Well, well, well... What have we here...? If it isn't my little runaway assistant...

ASSISTANT: *(Struggling for breath.)* You... you...!

YAMASHITA: *(Amused.)* I warned you about the Great Cabinet of GATT, didn't I? You shouldn't have gone in there without my permission.

ASSISTANT: *(Defiant, but still out-of-breath.)* The *women...*

YAMASHITA: *What* women?

ASSISTANT: The women who disappear. I *saw* where they went.

YAMASHITA: *(To the audience.)* How can you see women who have disappeared?

ASSISTANT: You know where they go.

YAMASHITA: They just disappear... It's magic! *(To the audience.)* Poof!

ASSISTANT: It's not magic. *(To the audience, still breathless.)* Call the police! Somebody call the police...

YAMASHITA: *(Indulgently.)* The police?

ASSISTANT: *(To audience.)* Call the police... she's part of a ring!

YAMASHITA: A ring?

ASSISTANT: *(Still out-of-breath.)* There's a man on the other side of the trick panel, and he tells the girls that he's going to give them a job, a better job than the one they have now... He says they can make thousands of dollars a month... that they can send the money back to their families... *(Suddenly, the FOURTH VOLUNTEER enters in the costume. The ASSISTANT reacts violently.)* No! No! Take that off!

YAMASHITA: *(Winking, to the FOURTH VOLUNTEER.)* Don't worry. She's my assistant. It's part of the show.

ASSISTANT: No! She's lying! Take those off!

FOURTH VOLUNTEER: *(Confused, to ASSISTANT.)* Why? *(To YAMASHITA.)* Wasn't I supposed to put this on?

YAMASHITA: *(To ASSISTANT.)* You're just confusing the girl. If you had been here, doing your job—

ASSISTANT: No! *(To VOLUNTEER.)* It's the costume—That's the trick! That's the trick! Don't you get it? Take it off!

YAMASHITA: I think my little assistant has been bitten by a certain green-eyed monster… You look lovely… *(To the audience.)*… doesn't she? *(Pause.)* Here she is, ladies and gentlemen… Let's have a big hand for—

ASSISTANT: *(Cutting her off.)* No! That's the trick!

FOURTH VOLUNTEER: What's the trick?

ASSISTANT: Cutting a woman in half! She fools you into putting on that shit, and she gets *them*… *(Indicating the audience.)* … to applaud, and then she gets you to take a bow, and that's how she does it! That's the trick!

YAMASHITA: *(Smiling, to the FOURTH VOLUNTEER.)* She's not making any sense, is she?

ASSISTANT: *(Frustrated.)* Yes, I am! It's like the costume splits you into two people…

YAMASHITA: First, you want us to believe you can see invisible women—

ASSISTANT: It's like you're outside yourself looking back in. That's what the costume does!

YAMASHITA: Well, thank you for making that clear—

ASSISTANT: And then she's going to make you disappear… or die… There isn't any magic! *(To the audience.)* There isn't any magic! She told you she was going to levitate someone didn't she? Look—! *(She pulls back the curtain to reveal an apparently unconscious SECOND VOLUNTEER.)* She's drugged! She's not levitating. She's *drugged*! *(Screaming.)* Don't you see? She's drugging and she's pimping and she's trafficking—(The STAGE MANAGER enters.)*

33

STAGE MANAGER: *(Cutting her off.)* What's going on?

YAMASHITA: *(Smiling.)* The Transnational Magic Show of the Millennia! *(Cymbals.)*

ASSISTANT: *(To STAGE MANAGER.)* No, there's no show. There's no magic! Yamashita has drugged *this* woman and she's going to pimp *that* woman!

STAGE MANAGER: *(Confused, to YAMASHITA.)* Is this part of the show?

YAMASHITA: *(Smiling.)* What do you think?

ASSISTANT: *(Frantic, pointing to SECOND VOLUNTEER.)* Look at her! She's unconscious! *(The STAGE MANAGER crosses to the woman and tries unsuccessfully to rouse her.)*

YAMASHITA: She's in a *trance.* I'm going to *levitate* her. That's the act. It's my little assistant who appears to be the one on drugs.

ASSISTANT: *(Speaking very rapidly.)* She's lying. She's trafficking! She trafficking the girls who go into the cabinet—That's why they never come back!

YAMASHITA: *(Pleasantly.)* But you went into the Cabinet, and you came back.

ASSISTANT: That's because I figured out the trick! *(To the STAGE MANAGER.)* Call the police! She's going to escape—

YAMASHITA: *(She is interrupted by a drum roll. YAMASHITA, laughing with delight, crosses the stage.)* Magic! Ladies and gentlemen... May I present... *(More drum roll.)* The Great Cabinet of GATT! *(She spins the Cabinet around and opens the door. A THAI GIRL of about fourteen steps out. She wears very trendy, designer clothing. She has an iPod and is talking on her cell phone. YAMASHITA addresses her.)* Excuse me... Excuse me! *(THAI GIRL stops her conversation and looks at her.)* Could you tell us about your job?

THAI GIRL: *(In Thai.) Garn-chao mee gum-nord sarm-sib pee... Bori-sut charm-gut nai pratayt tie... Sitee-keb-kin talord cheewit. Garn-chum-nong! Chanod-tee-din nor sor sam. khun süay mâak-mâak! Kii baat. Rong-rem-siam-you-tee-nay... mee-ahaan-mai-pet-mai... yaak-pai-rong-pai-abaan.*

Chop-maak tour-a-saap-moo-two! Chop-maak! (THAI GIRL goes back to her conversation.)

YAMASHITA: Translation: *(She imitates the girl.)* "Oh, my god... I make so much money. I have a scooter, and a cell phone, and I just bought an Ipod. And me and my girlfriend, we're moving into a new apartment. It's very beautiful. And we have all these cool clothes... I tell my girlfriends not to be stupid. They can make so much money. It's easy. So easy..."

ASSISTANT: No, it's not like that! *(She grabs the THAI GIRL's cell phone.)* It's not like that! Tell the truth!

THAI GIRL: *(Angry, grabbing it back.) Khor tom yum kung. Can tongkan bier neung kuat. Row ja mah ik krung. Mi phaen-thi thanon dee dee mai... Phom mi bal anuyat kup khi sakon. Chan soop buri dai mai. Phon tongkarn chao rot. Thang ork yu thi nai... Khun shui naeh-nam rong-raem hai noi. Pai rod-mei yu nai. Khun kao jai mai? Gun jerr phom high. Chai wella song cheumung. Phom mai bore!*

YAMASHITA: Translation... *(She imitates her again.)* "It *is* like that. My sister, she works in a soccer ball factory. She makes $118 a month. That's thirty dollars a week, or six dollars a day. I make more in one week than she makes in a whole month! And she works ten, twelve hours! I tell her she is stupid! She will never get anywhere. She will be a slave all her life. Me and my girlfriend, we are going to buy ourselves a house, and then an apartment. We are going to have our own business." *(Turning to THAI GIRL, YAMASHITA bows and thanks her in Thai) Cop coon kha. (She hands her several bills. The THAI GIRL smiles, takes the bills, and exits into the Cabinet. YAMASHITA turns to the STAGE MANAGER.)* That is the magic of GATT, my friend. The "General Agreement on Tariffs and Trade!" *(To the audience.)* Oh, surely everyone knows about GATT... The greatest feat of global fiscal prestidigitation ever performed... Eliminate trade restrictions and tariffs and—hey presto!—free markets! *(Laughing deliriously.) Free markets!* And thanks to the magic of GATT, our lovely Thai ambassador has figured out that her best prospects in life lie—so to speak—in a sector of the economy where demand is—shall we say—*perpetually elevated*! *(Crash of cymbals. She turns to the STAGE MANAGER.)* Satisfied?

STAGE MANAGER: *(Confused.)* So you're saying the girls go into the cabinet because they want to?

YAMASHITA: *(Smiling.)* It's referred to as "voluntary migration."

ASSISTANT: It's trafficking! It's prostitution! Those girls that go into that Cabinet of GATT, they never get out!

STAGE MANAGER: *(Suspicious, turning to YAMSHITA.)* Why don't you demonstrate how it works?

YAMASHITA: Very well... *(She turns to the FOURTH VOLUNTEER.)* Would you mind stepping into—

STAGE MANAGER: *(To YAMASHITA.)* No, not her —you!

YAMASHITA: I'm sorry...?

STAGE MANAGER: *You.*

ASSISTANT: Yeah! Get in it, bitch!

YAMASHITA: *(Ignoring her ASSISTANT, she turns in shock to the STAGE MANAGER.)* You want *me* to enter the Great Cabinet of GATT?

STAGE MANAGER: Voluntary migration. *(YAMASHITA hesitates.)*

YAMASHITA: *(Turning to the audience.)* And what about you? Do you want me to enter the Cabinet? *(Affirmative responses.)* Well, it seems I don't have a choice.

ASSISTANT: You got it. Feel the magic. *(With a show of reluctance, YAMASHITA enters the Cabinet. The ASSISTANT slams and locks the door. There is a moment of tense silence, followed by disturbingly realistic screaming, pleas for help, banging on the door, etc. as if a woman was actually being assaulted.)*

STAGE MANAGER: Is this part of the act?

ASSISTANT: *(Disturbed.)* I don't know.

STAGE MANAGER: *(Banging on the cabinet.)* Hey... hey! You okay in there?

YAMASHITA: *(Inside the cabinet.)* Help me! Please... help me! Oh, my god... Oh, no.... Help me... *(She continues to scream throughout the following dialogue.)*

STAGE MANAGER: *(To the ASSISTANT.)* Do you have a key?

36

ASSISTANT: *(Confused.)* No... Yamashita has the only key!

STAGE MANAGER: *(To the cabinet.)* This isn't funny! Come out! Come out of the cabinet!

YAMASHITA: *(Nearly incoherent.)* Please... oh, please... somebody...

STAGE MANAGER: I said come out! *(Suddenly, there is silence in the Cabinet. The STAGE MANAGER hesitates for a few seconds, and then takes the hammer from her toolbelt and smashes the lock. The door falls open and the body of YAMASHITA tumbles out. She is covered with blood. Nobody moves for a few seconds. Suddenly, YAMASHITA, from the floor, begins to laugh.)*

YAMASHITA: *(Rising.)* It's just a show... *It's all just a show!* (With a flourish, she tears off the bloody robe, revealing another spectacular outfit underneath. Using the bloody clothing, she wipes the blood from her face and hands.)*

STAGE MANAGER: *(Enraged.)* What do you think you're doing?

YAMASHITA: *(Wiping her face.)* You didn't know you were part of the show, did you?

STAGE MANAGER: You think this is funny?

YAMASHITA: Don't you?

STAGE MANAGER: *(Enraged.)* Okay, show's over. Get out of here. *(Shrugging, YAMASHITA begins to exit, and then turns suddenly.)*

YAMASHITA: Wait...! What's this?

STAGE MANAGER: *(Confused, she looks around.)* What?

YAMASHITA: Something... in your ear! *(Snapping her fingers, she appears to pull a rolled-up paper out of the STAGE MANAGER's ear.)* Why, it looks like some kind of a document... It's... a contract! A contract between... (Reading.)... the A-Mazing Yamashita and the [name of the theatre]. (Innocently, she hands it to the STAGE MANAGER.)*

ASSISTANT: It's another trick! Don't read it! Don't let her fool you!

YAMASHITA: *(To the STAGE MANAGER.)* It's not a trick. It's a legal contract, my friend… between your employer and myself. *(The STAGE MANAGER examines the document.)* If you attempt to interfere with my show any more, I will sue the management. *(Smiling.)* I will make your job disappear—poof! I will make your money disappear—poof! I will make your housing disappear—poof! And I think—yes, I believe—I will even make *you* disappear! *(The STAGE MANAGER, confused and angry, hesitates and then turns and exits. YAMASHITA laughs.)* Poof!

ASSISTANT: *(She tries to stop the STAGE MANAGER.)* No! Wait! Don't go! It's a trick… Come back! *(The STAGE MANAGER exits. YAMASHITA smiles at her ASSISTANT. The ASSISTANT turns to the audience.)* A cell phone! Somebody lend me their cell phone… *(The ASSISTANT must persist until someone in the audience gives her a phone. She takes it and appears to dial "911.")* Hello…? I want to report a crime… A woman has been drugged and she's unconscious… That's right… I don't know… They're going to kill her. Yeah… ambulance *and* police. Yeah, she's here. Yeah. [Address of the theatre]. *(She returns the phone.)* Yeah. I'm watching you, bitch.

YAMASHITA: I hope so. *(Turning to the FOURTH VOLUNTEER, who has been standing uncomfortably to the side.)* But you are confused, aren't you? You can't tell what's real and what isn't, can you? *(To the audience.)* Isn't that the mark of a good magician…? *(To the FOURTH VOLUNTEER.)* But I tell you what I'm going to do. I'm going to explain the secret of all my tricks to you, and you are going to share them with the audience. How about that…? But of course, you don't have to share them if you don't want to. You don't have to do anything that you don't want to. What did I just say?

FOURTH VOLUNTEER: *(Confused.)* I don't have to do anything I don't want to.

YAMASHITA: What?

FOURTH VOLUNTEER: I don't have to do anything I don't want to.

YAMASHITA: I hope not… I have these brochures…? *(She pulls out a stack from a pocket. These are actually downloads from the World Trade Organization website.)* Go ahead… touch them! *(YAMASHITA holds out a stack. The VOLUNTEER touches them.)* They're real, aren't they? They're not magic… And do you know what these are?

FOURTH VOLUNTEER: No…

YAMASHITA: They're brochures that explain all of my tricks. That's right... They explain all of my tricks... how they work. And I am going to do something that no magician in the world has ever done before! I am going to share the secrets of my magic with the audience, and you are going to help me... if you want to. *Only* if you want to. *(A long pause.)*

FOURTH VOLUNTEER: What do I do?

YAMASHITA: Well, you take these brochures... Here—take them all... *(Handing them to her.)*... and you will pass them out to the members of the audience.

FOURTH VOLUNTEER: Can I put my clothes back on?

YAMASHITA: You mean change out of your costume?

FOURTH VOLUNTEER: Yes.

YAMASHITA: Why would you want to do that? The costume is part of the show! If you aren't wearing the costume, you can't be part of the show, can you? And if you're not part of the show, you can't help the audience understand the magic, and you said you wanted to do that, didn't you? *(Silence.)* Besides, I think they like the way you look in your costume... And why wouldn't they? You're a beautiful woman. Is it their fault if they appreciate that? You don't want to make them feel ashamed, do you? *(After a pause, the FOURTH VOLUNTEER takes the brochures and crosses down in the theatre, where she moves awkwardly among the audience handing out the brochures. YAMASHITA addresses the audience.)* Yamashita knows what you are thinking. You are thinking, "The assistant is right! There are one hundred and thirteen million women and girls every year who are missing... This cannot be just a trick! One hundred and thirteen *million* women and girls who are missing from female infanticide, trafficking, death in childbirth from inadequate medical care, disproportionate neglect as children, infections from female genital mutilation, "honor killings" and "dowry deaths"... every year? Your head is breaking open with the weight of this oppression—and you are worried about this woman who is going to levitate—is it *really* a trance, or has she been drugged...? And you are worried about my angry little assistant— where did she go and will the police really come...? And you are even worried about the woman who has volunteered to hand out the brochures that explain all my tricks, because she has stopped doing her job... look! *(The FOURTH VOLUNTEER has stopped handing out brochures and is cringing against a side wall in the theatre.)* So much to worry about... Is it real, or is it just an illusion? But let's call in a professor to help us, shall we? Let's call in a professor from a big university, and perhaps she will help us figure this out... *(YAMASHITA claps her hands, and a PROFESSOR YESSIR appears. She is a middle-class, middle-aged white woman—cautious and arrogant.)* Professor Yessir! Welcome to the Transnational Magic Show of the Millennium!

PROFESSOR YESSIR: Thank you... It's a great privilege to be here.

YAMASHITA: Now, Professor Yessir, we have invited you here, because there are some in the audience who do not believe this is a show.

PROFESSOR YESSIR: Ah.

YAMASHITA: Yes. So I thought that you might be able to speak to their concern.

PROFESSOR YESSIR: Which is?

YAMASHITA: Which is "the women."

PROFESSOR YESSIR: *(Stalling.)* "The women..." Yes...

YAMASHITA: I thought you might be willing to take questions from the audience.

PROFESSOR YESSIR: Ah... The audience...

YAMASHITA: Them. *(Indicating the audience.)*

PROFESSOR YESSIR: Ah, yes... "Them."

YAMASHITA: So, Professor, would you be willing to answer some questions?

PROFESSOR YESSIR: *(Clarifying.)* From "them?"

YAMASHITA: Yes. *(The PROFESSOR YESSIR turns expectantly toward the audience. YAMASHITA addresses the audience.)* Go ahead... Ask the Professor! Tell *her* what's bothering you... *(A WOMAN raises her hand.)*

PROFESSOR YESSIR: Yes. You there...

WOMAN: *(Rising.)* What happens to the women? *(YAMASHITA and the PROFESSOR YESSIR exchange a knowing look.)*

PROFESSOR YESSIR: *(Indulgently.)* Ah, well… first we need to establish what you mean by "the women."

WOMAN: The women who are missing.

PROFESSOR YESSIR: No, what do you mean when you use the word "women?"

WOMAN: Women?

PROFESSOR YESSIR: Yes, "women." To whom do you refer when you say "women?"

WOMAN: *(Confused.)* Females.

PROFESSOR YESSIR: Meaning?

WOMAN: Females… Women… Women and girls. *(YAMASHITA and the PROFESSOR YESSIR exchange another look.)* Humans with double-X chromosomes…

PROFESSOR YESSIR: *(Smiling indulgently.)* But what about double-XY or triple-X? Are *they* women? On estimate, at least 4% of humans have a chromosomal karotype other than XX or XY—

WOMAN: *(Annoyed, the WOMAN cuts her off.)* People with breasts and uteruses.

PROFESSOR YESSIR: *(Excited by the chase.)* So that would *not* include those with hysterectomies or mastectomies? Or would you count implants? And if you do, then, of course—

WOMAN: *(Frustrated.)* You know what I'm talking about! The female sex!

PROFESSOR YESSIR: I think you mean "gender," not "sex."

WOMAN: All right, "gender!"

PROFESSOR YESSIR: *(Victory.)* Ah. *(Reciting.)* "There is no gender identity behind the expressions of gender… Identity is performatively constituted by the very 'expressions' that are said to be its results." Judith Butler.

YAMASHITA: Poof!

WOMAN: I don't know what you're talking about, but I want to know *what happened* to the women.

PROFESSOR YESSIR: "... a woman cannot 'be'; it is something which does not even belong in the order or being. It follows that a feminist practice can only be negative, at odds with what already exists so that we may say 'that's not it' and 'that's still not it.'" Julia Kristeva.

YAMASHITA: Poof!

WOMAN: *(Increasingly frustrated.) What?*

PROFESSOR YESSIR: *(Triumphant.)* "The Woman does not exist!" Jacques Lacan.

YAMASHITA: Poof! Thank you, Professor—

WOMAN: Wait a minute! You didn't answer my question!

PROFESSOR YESSIR: I didn't need to... I deconstructed it! *(Crash of cymbals. Just then voices are heard offstage, and the ASSISTANT runs in, pointing at YAMASHITA.)*

ASSISTANT: There she is! That's her! That's her! *(An OFFICER and an EMERGENCY MEDICAL TECHNICIAN enter. The EMT is wheeling a gurney. PROFESSOR YESSIR quickly, but unobtrusively takes a seat in the audience.)* And here's the woman who has been drugged... *(The EMT begins to check the vital signs of the SECOND VOLUNTEER. YAMASHITA opens the door of the Cabinet of GATT. The ASSISTANT sees this.)* No! Stop her! Don't let her go into the cabinet! She's trying to escape! *(The OFFICER crosses quickly to YAMASHITA, who steps to the side of the cabinet, inviting him to inspect it. The ASSISTANT crosses to them.)* She gets them to go in there, and then she locks the door—

YAMASHITA: ... and I make them disappear in plain view of an audience. All very criminal, as you can see.

ASSISTANT: It is!

EMT: *(Calling suddenly to the ASSISTANT.)* Can you help me with her? We need to get her on the gurney. *(The ASSISTANT crosses back to the*

SECOND VOLUNTEER and helps lift her onto the gurney. As she is doing this, YAMASHITA is quietly counting bills out for the OFFICER.)

ASSISTANT: *(Unaware of the payoff, she turns back to the OFFICER.)* Don't let her get away! I can prove it! *(The OFFICER crosses to the ASSISTANT.)*

OFFICER: You were a witness?

ASSISTANT: Yes, sir. I saw everything. After the show—

OFFICER: It's a show?

ASSISTANT: No...

OFFICER: But you just said—

ASSISTANT: No, but *after*—

OFFICER: After what?

ASSISTANT: After the women disappeared, I followed them... I saw what—*(The EMT begins to wheel the gurney toward the Cabinet.)* Wait! Stop! What are you doing? You can't take her in there! She needs to go to the hospital! *(Suddenly, the OFFICER pulls the ASSISTANT's arms back and clamps a pair of handcuffs on her.)* What? No! It's Yamashita! She's the one! This is a mistake... *(The EMT has already entered the cabinet. The OFFICER frog-marches the ASSISTANT into the Cabinet.)* No! No! Wait! You've got the wrong person. No! *(Shoving the ASSISTANT ahead of him, the OFFICER climbs into the cabinet also, turns, and tips his hat to YAMASHITA, who slams the door shut. She uses the STAGE MANAGER's hammer to bolt the door. Turning suddenly back to the audience, she spots the FOURTH VOLUNTEER, who is still frozen against a wall of the theatre.)*

YAMASHITA: What do you think you're doing, you little slut? Just standing there! And what are you staring at? Are you concerned about your friends in the Cabinet? Would you like to join them...? No...? Then I suggest you get to work! And since you're so fond of standing in one place, you can go stand outside the theatre and get people to buy tickets for the show. Go on! Get out of here! And if you try to run away, I'll have the officer arrest you for stealing the costume. Get to work! *Now! (The FOURTH VOLUNTEER exits quickly. After she is gone, YAMASHITA laughs pleasantly, turning to the audience.)* Just part of the show, folks...

43

part of the show! *(A brief pause.)* I know that you know she's really just an actor... Because, after all, you're the audience. But now it is time for my final trick... And Professor Yessir is going to assist me... aren't you...? *(She looks into the audience. PROFESSOR YESSIR rises and crosses to the stage. She pulls a curtain or flips a switch that produces a screen.)* Some of you are very uncomfortable, aren't you...? I know you are, but we are going to fix that... *(To PROFESSOR YESSIR.)*... aren't we? *(To the audience.)* I'm going to hypnotize you. That's right. The A-Mazing Yamashita is going to put all of you into a trance—Not just one, or even two of you... or even a dozen!—but the entire theatre at the same time! And this will not be a party trick! No! The A-Mazing Yamashita is not going make you believe that you are a chicken! She is not going to make you believe that you have been burned by the touch of an ice cube! No, the A-Mazing Yamashita is going to put you into a trance that will transform your life! Now, I know some of you are thinking, "How can that be? How can a mere magician on a stage change my life?" Because this is not just magic. It's science! Isn't that right, Professor? *(PROFESSOR YESSIR smiles.)* Yamashita is going to work with your brain chemistry! Your brain will be doing the magic all by itself. *You* will be the magic! And this is possible, because of science... ladies and gentlemen... neurophysiology. When two neurons fire at the same time, they connect. That's it. That's all it takes. It's called an "association." Your brain is going to make the associations for you, and all you have do is call up the images and you will re-experience the trance. And these will not be just ordinary associations, like when you look out the window and see that it's raining so you reach for an umbrella. You don't need any help with associations like those. No, the A-Mazing Yamashita is going to take two entirely opposite things, things that, without magic, your brain would never learn to associate, and Yamashita is going to give your brain an opportunity to forge a permanent synaptic link between them. Ladies and gentlemen... picture this! What if every time you began to feel the pain of humiliation, you could convert that to a delicious sense of mounting excitement? What if every time you started to suffer empathetically with the agony of another, you could convert that to an intense sensation of exquisite pleasure? What if... instead of that helpless sense of overwhelming rage and frustration in the face of tyranny, you could transform it instantly to an overwhelmingly intoxicating awareness of personal empowerment? And what if these linkages would remain with you, structurally and neurochemically, forever? Forever, ladies and gentlemen... because, tonight, for my final and greatest feat of magic, the A-Mazing Yamashita is going to... *(Drum roll.)*... make inequality sexy! *(Cymbals crash.)* That's right... I am going to *make inequality sexy!* *(Cymbals. She turns to the PROFESSOR YESSIR.)* Are you ready? *(The PROFESSOR YESSIR nods. A screen descends.)* Then *let the show begin!* *(Another cymbal.)* And now, ladies and gentlemen, I ask you to suspend your judgment, because a narrow, judgmental perspective will inhibit the brain's freedom to form these synaptic links. Instead, I ask you to focus your full attention on the screen before you and on the images that I am going to show you. *(An image of a naked woman is displayed fleetingly. Suddenly, the screen goes dark.)* What's wrong? Where is the picture?

STAGE MANAGER: *(Entering.)* There aren't going to be any pictures. I pulled the plug on your little show.

YAMASHITA: You can't do that.

STAGE MANAGER: It's pornography, isn't it?

YAMASHITA: *(Shaking her head.)* It is a series of selected representations of erotic imagery.

STAGE MANAGER: It's pornography. It's men dominating and degrading women. It's white men over women of color. It's adults over children—

YAMASHITA: *(Cutting her off, and turning to the PROFESSOR.)* Professor...?

PROFESSOR YESSIR: Yes... "The trauma of the Sixties persuaded me that my generation's egalitarianism was a sentimental error. I now see the hierarchical as both beautiful and necessary. Efficiency liberates; egalitarianism tangles, delays, blocks, deadens." Camille Paglia.

STAGE MANAGER: *(To YAMASHITA.)* You're not going to show that here.

YAMASHITA: *(To STAGE MANAGER.)* This is censorship. You are interfering with my freedom of speech, and that is a constitutional right.

STAGE MANAGER: Hey... you know what? What about their freedom of speech? These are pictures of real acts being done to real people.

YAMASHITA: It's called "consent."

STAGE MANAGER: Yeah... "consent." Unh-hunh. *(To PROFESSOR YESSIR.)* Hey, there's a job for you... Why don't you try deconstructing something really useful like "consent?" Why don't you tell us what that means when the alternatives are losing your children or starving?

YAMASHITA: *(Smiling, to PROFESSOR YESSIR.)* Go ahead, Professor...

PROFESSOR YESSIR: "... a power relationship can only be articulated on the basis of two elements which are each indispensable if it is really to be a power relationship—

STAGE MANAGER: What the hell...?

YAMASHITA: Wait!

PROFESSOR YESSIR: *(Continuing.)*"... that 'the other'—the one over whom power is exercised—be thoroughly recognized and maintained to the very end as a person who acts; and that, faced with a relationship of power, a whole field of responses, reactions, results, and possible inventions may open up." Michel Foucault

STAGE MANAGER: *(Pausing in disbelief, to the PROFESSOR YESSIR.)* You're a fucking idiot. You know that? *(To YAMASHITA.)* Get out of here! Both of you!

YAMASHITA: Who is going to make me? The police are on my side. The doctors are on my side. The academics are on my side. I think you will find that there is no one who can enforce my eviction.

STAGE MANAGER: *They* can. *(Indicating the audience.)*

YAMASHITA: Them? Oh, I don't think so. They have paid their money to see the show. I think you will find that they want their money's worth. *(The STAGE MANAGER hesitates.)* Shall we see? *(The STAGE MANAGER says nothing. YAMASHITA turns to the audience.)* My friends, do you want me to continue? *(If the audience objects, the STAGE MANAGER turns to YAMASHITA.)**

STAGE MANAGER: Okay... That's it. The show's over. *(Suddenly, there is a flash of light, and YAMASHITA disappears in a cloud of smoke. The STAGE MANAGER turns to the audience.)* Any volunteers to help me take this Cabinet thing apart? Yes? Just come on up here... *(As her volunteers start to mount the stage, the STAGE MANAGER starts to take out her hammer.)* See...that's how it works... No audience, no show... *(To the PROFESSOR YESSIR.)* Quote that! *(She starts taking apart the Cabinet as the house lights come up.)*

Blackout

End of Play

*ALTERNATE ENDING:

[If the audience does *not* object to the slideshow.]

STAGE MANAGER: Well, I'm going to walk out. And I invite any of you who are uncomfortable to walk out with me, because this is bullshit. *(She exits and the slideshow continues for another five minutes with increasingly pornographic images. At the end of it, YAMASHITA speaks.)*

YAMASHITA: And now... ladies and gentlemen... when I clap my hands, you will return to your normal state of consciousness. *(She claps her hands.)* Thank you, thank you all... Professor...? I hope you enjoyed our little show... Please tell all your friends... *(The PROFESSOR steps forward and together they take a bow.)*

The Rules of the Playground

A Play in One Act

The Rules of the Playground

A Play in One Act

Five women, all mothers, have gathered in a classroom of their children's middle school to take part in an experimental, new program designed to eliminate playground violence. Experts from international "think tanks" and peacekeeping forces are training the women on how to analyze playground dynamics in order to detect the class, ethnic, and racial inequalities among the children that are, in theory, the sources of conflict. The program's focus is emphatically on confronting social imbalances, not individual behaviors, and, to facilitate this focus, the women have been forbidden to look out the window at the playground. In fact, the blinds are shut.

An enthusiastic newcomer joins the group, but her enthusiasm changes to confusion as it is revealed that, a week earlier, one child was shot on the playground and another was raped. The newcomer reacts with disbelief and then alarm, as the sounds of gunfire and screaming are heard from the playground.

This is a scathing social satire, along the lines of Shirley Jackson's electrifying short story "The Lottery." *The Rules of the Playground* demonstrates how the everyday social conditioning of women is exploited in order to perpetuate denial and compliance.

Six women
Twenty-five minutes
Single set

Cast of Characters

MADELEINE: A mother, 35-50.

JEANNE: A mother, 35-50.

MARGARET: A mother, 35-50.

GOLDIE: A mother, 35-50.

INDIRA: A mother, 35-50.

SHELLEY: A mother, 35-50.

Scene

A classroom in a middle school.

Time

The present.

Ethnicity Chart

	MONDAY	TUESDAY	WEDNESDAY	THURSDAY	FRIDAY
BB HOOP	AA	AsA	PRA	MA/H	EA
MONKEY BARS	AsA	PRA	MA/H	EA	AA
SWINGS	PRA	MA/H	EA	AA	AsA
TREES	MA/H	EA	AA	AsA	PRA
PICNIC TABLES	EA	AA	AsA	PRA	MA/H

AA—African American
AsA—Asian American
EA—European American
MA/H—Mexican American/ Hispanic
PRA—Puerto Rican American

Map of the Playground

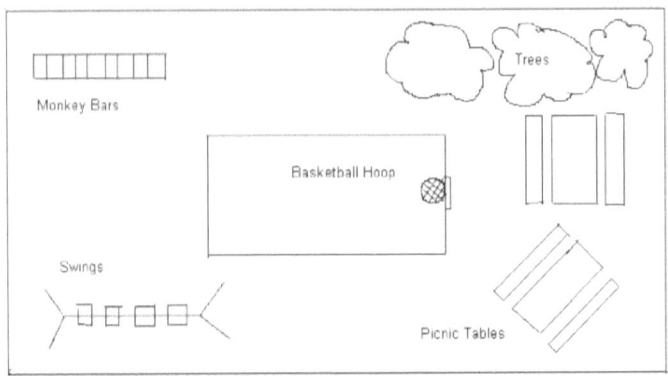

The Rules of the Playground

The interior of a middle school classroom. There are rows of windows, with blinds or curtains, along the back wall. These windows look out over the playground. At the start of the play, all of the blinds have been pulled down, completely obscuring the view of the playground. Up left are two large easels. One displays the "Ethnicity Chart," and the other supports a large dry board with the map of the playground. Downstage left is the doorway into the classroom from the hall. Down right is a small table with a coffeemaker, sugar, cups, etc. Rows of chairs, or chairs with desks are in the center of the stage, facing left. The classroom is empty. MADELEINE enters carrying her copy of the "PDA Handbook." (All of the women except SHELLEY will have a copy of this.) MADELEINE is uneasy. She sets her handbook on one of the chairs and crosses to the coffee pot. She is pouring herself a cup of coffee when JEANNE enters. Startled, MADELEINE spills her coffee.

MADELEINE: *(Distracted, as she tries to clean up the spill using napkins.)* Jeanne... *(JEANNE, who has crossed purposefully to one of the chairs, is busy with her notebook and purse.)* I... I didn't expect to see you here...

JEANNE: *(All business.)* Why not? *(MADELEINE does not know what to say.)* I think it's even more important for me to be here now.

MADELEINE: You're right. I wasn't thinking... Can I get you some coffee?

JEANNE: No, thank you. *(She seats herself in the front row, facing the easels.)*

MADELEINE: *(Fishing.)* It's certainly challenging to change the way we think about things...

JEANNE: *(Turning.)* And how are *you* doing?

MADELEINE: Oh... I... Well... It's been a hard week... But not as hard as yours.

JEANNE: *(Sternly.)* There's no way to compare the two experiences. *(Suddenly noticing the blinds/curtains.)* Why are the blinds [curtains] up?

MADELEINE: *(Panicked.)* Oh! I didn't realize they were...

JEANNE: Did you look?

MADELEINE: *(Backing up toward the window.)* No... No, I haven't been near the window. *(Closing the blinds/curtains without facing them.)* It must have been from last week... when I heard the... you know...when the... *(She checks herself and lapses into silence. There is a pause.)*

JEANNE: How *is* your daughter?

MADELEINE: *(Retreating to a seat at the back of the classroom.)* Oh...well...we've both been working very hard. It hasn't been easy, dislodging stereotypes... Especially about gender...

JEANNE: Yes.

MADELEINE: Really? You, too? I would have thought—

JEANNE: *(Cutting her off.)* Of course. *(A beat.)* Is she on the playground? Did you bring her?

MADELEINE: *(Long pause.)* She's at home. *(JEANNE looks at her. MADELEINE is very uncomfortable.)* I'm hoping she'll decide to come next week... *(Embarrassed.)* I'd rather the others didn't know that she didn't come today... *(Just then MARGARET enters with artificial briskness. She marches straight over to the coffee, pretending not to see JEANNE. JEANNE and MADELEINE have a strong and immediate response to her presence. They look away from her.)*

MARGARET: *(Greeting MADELEINE, who is sitting close to the table.)* Good morning. *(MADELEINE turns, but does not say anything.)* That was a wonderful workshop last week, wasn't it? It's all about focus, isn't it? I just got so much out of it—didn't you? *(MADELEINE turns away. MARGARET, pretending to ignore this, turns to survey the classroom.)* I wonder where the trainer is...?

JEANNE: It's early.

MARGARET: *(Pretending to notice JEANNE for the first time.)* Oh... Jeanne! What a surprise to see you!

JEANNE: *(Not taken in by MARGARET's performance.)* And why is it a surprise?

MARGARET: *(Attempting to patronize her.)* Well, really, there's no need for you to be here now.

JEANNE: *(Rising.)* I think there's very much a need… *"now."*

MARGARET: Well, it *is* a workshop for *parents.*

MADELEINE: Jeanne is still a parent.

GOLDIE: *(Just then GOLDIE enters with a plate of brownies covered with plastic wrap. She gasps when she sees JEANNE.)* Jeanne! I am so glad to see you! *(She crosses to hug her. JEANNE receives the embrace with stiff formality.)* I wanted to call you, but I wasn't sure if it would be okay...after what they said at the workshop about "focus" and everything.... But here you are, and I'm so glad to see you! How are you? *(JEANNE doesn't respond.)*

MADELEINE: Jeanne feels it's important to finish the training.

GOLDIE: Well, good for you! And we're glad you're here! *(She hugs her again and then looks around.)* I made us some brownies for the workshop today. I thought it might be nice to have a little something to nibble on, along with our coffee.

MADELEINE: This isn't a tea party.

GOLDIE: *(Crossing to the chair in front of MADELEINE.)* Oh, my god! Oh, Madeleine! I am *so* sorry… I had forgotten completely… I was just so glad to see Jeanne here after what happened last week... I totally forgot about your Christy! How is she?

MADELEINE: We're working with it.

GOLDIE: Oh, bless her heart! I know she's being so brave. What a little soldier! I certainly didn't mean any disrespect. If you think it's inappropriate to have the brownies here, I can just put them out in my car… It's not a problem at all. They were just kind of a little spur-of-the moment thing… I just really didn't think—

MARGARET: *(Crossing aggressively to GOLDIE.)* I'll have one. *(GOLDIE breaks off and turns to look at MARGARET for the first time since she entered.)* I didn't have any breakfast. *(There's an awkward pause. GOLDIE unwraps a corner of the plate and holds the dish out to MARGARET. MARGARET peels back the rest of the plastic to survey all the brownies. She takes two and bites into one.)* Mmm… delicious. *(MARGARET crosses back to the last row and sits by MADELEINE. GOLDIE turns apologetically toward JEANNE and MADELEINE, embarrassed to be feeding the enemy. She places the brownies on an empty chair. Just then INDIRA enters with SHELLEY.)*

INDIRA: *(To SHELLEY.)* Oh, good—we're still early. *(To the others.)* Hello, ladies—I want you all to meet Shelley. *(They all turn to look at her.)* She's new to the district.

SHELLEY: I just moved here…

INDIRA: They told her she was too late to get into the program, because she had already missed the first session, but Shelley wouldn't take "no" for an answer, so here she is! They asked me to do the introductions…

GOLDIE: Hi, Shelley. Welcome to the program. I'm Goldie.

MADELEINE: Madeleine.

MARGARET: *(Sourly.)* Margaret. *(A silence.)*

INDIRA: And this is Jeanne.

SHELLEY: *(Oblivious to the tension in the room, SHELLEY waxes enthusiastic.)* Well, I just thought it was so wonderful to see a middle-school so committed to eliminating violence—and not just in a kind of window-dressing way—but to have such a commitment that they bring this kind of program in—I mean international peacekeeping experts from some of the biggest think tanks in the country, coming here—to a *middle school*—to analyze what's happening on the playground like it was some kind of international conflict… I mean to take it so *seriously*, what happens with children, as if the world depended on it—which it *does*, because *this* is where it all starts… right here… I mean, this is just so *radical*! And *then*, to focus on the *mothers* for the training… It's just so *refreshing* to see a program that acknowledges the fact that we *are* the primary caregivers and that our influence is really unique. I just really appreciate that, because I'm a single mother. *(She pauses.)* Is anyone else here a single mom?

GOLDIE: *(Eager to redeem herself.)* Jeanne—*(There is an awkward silence. GOLDIE, with horror, realizes her mistake.)*

JEANNE: *(Turning around.)* I *was* a single mother. My son is dead.

SHELLEY: Oh, I'm sorry.

JEANNE: My son died as a result of playground violence, and that's why I'm here. *(She looks at MARGARET, who ignores her.)*

SHELLEY: Was it recent?

JEANNE: Last week.

MARGARET: Well, I think we may need to catch Shelley up on some of what she missed. *(To SHELLEY.)* Did they tell you anything about the first session? *(SHELLEY, still staring at JEANNE, turns.)* Did they tell you what you missed?

SHELLEY: No.

MARGARET: "Focus." *(Pointing with two fingers from her eyes to SHELLEY's eyes, the "focus gesture")*

SHELLEY: What?

MARGARET: The subject of last week's session… "Focus." *(Repeating the gesture.)*

SHELLEY: Oh.

GOLDIE: Yes. Focus is very important. I took a lot of notes. *(Checking her notes.)* You see, we mothers have really been trained in another direction. It's not our fault or anything, but it's just that, because we have had to change diapers, cook breakfast, make the beds, see that the socks match—although I don't do that, because, honestly, who is going to notice the socks on a twelve-year-old boy—*(JEANNE glares at GOLDIE.)*—but, anyway, we have not learned to focus on the big picture.

INDIRA: Can't see the woods for the trees…

MARGARET: Can't see the war for the bandages.

GOLDIE: Yes. That's just what the trainer said: Women can't see the war for the bandages. So the first thing we have to do is learn to focus on the right thing.

SHELLEY: *(Intrigued.)* And what is the right thing?

INDIRA: The rules of the playground. *(She gestures toward the dry board.)* This is a diagram of the playground.

SHELLEY: What playground?

GOLDIE: The one right here, right outside the windows… Where we drop the children off.

INDIRA: And you can see that it's all divided up into 'safety zones"—

MADELEINE: *(Interrupting, she turns to SHELLEY.)* Do you have a daughter?

MARGARET: *(Jumping in.)* That doesn't make any difference.

GOLDIE: *(Anxiously, to SHELLEY.)* That's right. Gender is not the issue. *(To MARGARET, apologetically.)* That's been one of the hardest attitudes to change.

MADELEINE: *(To SHELLEY.)* Do you have a daughter?

INDIRA: Why are you asking her that?

MADELEINE: Because I think she ought to know.

SHELLEY: Know what?

INDIRA: *(Quickly.)* You ought to know that this program is one hundred percent committed to eradicating stereotypes about gender—*(To MADELEINE.)* All stereotypes. There is no room in this program for any misogyny *or* for any male-bashing—or any racism, anti-Semitism, heterosexism—There is absolutely no room for prejudice of any kind in the rules of the playground.

SHELLEY: *(With visible relief.)* Well, I'm all for that. *(To MADELEINE.)* I *do* have a daughter, but I'm raising her to be a feminist. *(She sits in the front row.)*

MARGARET: *(Ominously.)* The trainer spent quite a little time last week talking about feminism.

SHELLEY: That's wonderful!

INDIRA: I don't know if "wonderful" is the word. I mean, we're grateful to the feminists for what they've done to raise awareness about inequality toward women—but their lack of political experience—which was not their fault—has led to a painful legacy of prejudice against males, so that now, two generations later, we are reaping the bitter harvest of those seeds of hatred planted by the feminists.

MARGARET: That's right.

GOLDIE: *(Earnestly.)* A lot of people want to blame violence in the schools on boys, but it's that very attitude that makes them act out.

SHELLEY: *(Turning.)* I don't understand. Isn't it mostly men who are fighting the wars and doing the raping and killing—

MARGARET: *(Furiously.)* Focus!

INDIRA: *(Crossing to the board.)* Okay… *(Tapping the board to get their attention.)* The safety zones… These have been scientifically drawn up to address the inequalities inherent in any population of children—or adults.

SHELLEY: *(Confused.)* What do you mean?

INDIRA: Well… for example, this area here is considered one of the "preferred safety zones," because of the desirability of playing basketball. These… *(Pointing.)*… the monkey bars, the area with the trees, the picnic tables—these are all preferred zones also. Similar to, say, countries with oil fields. These preferred zones are on a rotation system. No one group of children can monopolize them.

SHELLEY: Wait a minute—what "groups" of children are you talking about?

GOLDIE: *(Checking her handbook.)* In this particular school, we have about 40% African American, 15% Latino, 35% European-American, and 10% "other." Now, the breakdown by income is 30% low income, 40% middle class, which would be, for a two-parent family, over $50,000 a year… Then, you've got the Catholics and the Protestants and the Jews—

SHELLEY: *(To GOLDIE.)* But I thought you didn't discriminate!

INDIRA: We don't. But we don't put our heads in the sand either. These are populations that have either common cultures, or who face common oppressions… *outside* the school, of course. And we want to honor their affinities and their cultural identities and acknowledge their disadvantages by assigning them their own safety zones on the playground. And, as you can see... *(Indicating the formulas.)* ... this is a complicated process. But we have a team of some of the world's most experienced political analysts and peacekeepers to instruct us in how to do that.

GOLDIE: Yes. The safety zones are the cornerstone of the whole peacekeeping program.

MARGARET: Boundaries.

SHELLEY: But it sounds like the children can't play together...

INDIRA: No, no, no! The safety zones don't restrict them! They just give them a power base from which they can learn to negotiate shared use with others. For instance... *(Pointing to the "Ethnicity Chart.")* ... today is Monday. As you can see on the "Ethnicity Chart," the African-American students have the basketball safety zone today... Now, they can use their temporary control of that area to negotiate with, say, the Asian-American children for the use of the monkey bars... or, with the European-American children for the picnic tables...but, if they choose not to share—and that's their choice—well, as you can see, tomorrow the Asian Americans will have the basketball hoop and the African Americans the picnic tables.

GOLDIE: On traditional playgrounds, with no safety zones, the dominant group controls everything all the time.

INDIRA: We are giving everyone a piece of the pie right from the start. They don't have to fight for it.

SHELLEY: But it's so complicated... When are the children going to have time to play?

MADELEINE: *(Cryptically.)* You mean, "fight?"

GOLDIE: *(Hastily.)* So how did your former school handle conflict?

SHELLEY: *(To MADELEINE.)* What do you mean, "fight?"

INDIRA: Yes, Shelley, how did your old school handle conflict? This was one of the questions they asked all of us in last week's workshop.

MARGARET: The one you missed.

SHELLEY: *(Standing to address the group.)* Oh... Well, I guess we would give the kids "time out" if they were being inappropriate.

MARGARET: *(Sneering.)* "Inappropriate!"

SHELLEY: *(Confused by MARGARET's hostility.)* You know, where you send the child off to be by himself...

MARGARET: "*Him*self?"

SHELLEY: Yes... Until he's ready to rejoin the others...

MARGARET: "He?"

INDIRA: *Or* "she."

GOLDIE: We used to have timeouts here, too, before the peacekeeper program.

INDIRA: It's blaming the children.

SHELLEY: What is?

INDIRA: Timeouts.

SHELLEY: I don't understand.

GOLDIE: We have to *completely* change the way we think.

INDIRA: The timeouts and the locker checks and the detention halls—these are just ways of scapegoating the children. It's really *inequality* that's behind the violence. You solve the problem of inequality and you remove the motive for acting out.

GOLDIE: *(Reading from the handbook.)* "Timeouts and detention just humiliate the child, sowing seeds of frustration and revenge that will yield a bitter harvest of violence down the road."

SHELLEY: But what if the child is being inappropriate—

MARGARET: *(Cutting her off.)* Children are *always* appropriate. *(SHELLEY stares at her.)*

GOLDIE: That's right. If we mothers don't like what they're doing, it's up to us to locate the inequality that is the source of their frustration and adjust the rules. *(She smiles.)* Focus. *(The "focus" gesture.)*

SHELLEY: What if whatever they're doing is just because they're tired or cranky or because they saw it on TV—

GOLDIE: Oh, no! We can't blame TV!

SHELLEY: But there have been studies that television and video games—

MARGARET: You can prove anything with studies. But if you really want to solve a problem, you go to the experts.

INDIRA: And have we got experts! Listen… We've got folks here from the Middle East, from Northern Ireland, from Afghanistan… Rwanda… *(JEANNE, still standing at the back of the classroom, kicks the trashcan. The others turn to look at her. There is an awkward silence.)*

SHELLEY: But do these rules of the playground really work? *(JEANNE laughs. Another silence.)*

INDIRA: *(Uncomfortable with JEANNE's outbursts.)* Well, it takes time for any new system to take root, but, yes, absolutely. And at the end of the ten weeks of this program, all of us here will be certified PDA's.

GOLDIE: "Playground Dynamics Analysts."

INDIRA: We will all be competent to evaluate what we see on the playground and adjust the safety zones to respond to any crisis.

SHELLEY: You mean, you never discipline the children?

INDIRA: The PDA *observes*, but never interferes.

GOLDIE: *(Reading from the handbook.)* "It is imperative, in order to maintain neutrality, that the peacekeeper respect the process of all parties. The role of the PDA is limited to analysis and interpretation of violence, and allocation of safety zones."

SHELLEY: So you treat the playground as if it was the world, and the children represent all of the different nations competing for resources…

GOLDIE: Exactly!

SHELLEY: And the children will not be disciplined, because they will be treated like adults.

MARGARET: Discipline only humiliates them.

GOLDIE: *(Reading.)* "When you discipline a child, he or she internalizes the blame, which destroys the impulse toward social justice."

SHELLEY: But if a child is getting hurt by other children—

MADELEINE: *(Cutting in.)* We let them do it.

MARGARET: *(Attempting to divert attention from MADELEINE.)* Focus! It's about focus!

SHELLEY: But what about the child?

MARGARET: I think it is really a mistake for anyone who missed that first session to be allowed to join the program.

JEANNE: *(Responding to SHELLEY.)* That child should know how to fight. *(There is a silence, and then all the women begin to speak at once.)*

GOLDIE: That's not the point…

INDIRA: The big picture! We have to look at the big picture!

MARGARET: I don't see why they decided to set aside their own rules to let someone…

MADELEINE: *(Endorsing JEANNE.)* That's right! That's right!

JEANNE: *Quiet! (The women stop talking. JEANNE crosses slowly to the front of the class.)* My son is dead. Margaret's two boys killed him last week while the blinds were down [curtains were closed] and our international peacekeeping expert-of-the-day stood and watched.

GOLDIE: *(Nervous.)* I think we should wait for the PDA before we try to analyze what happened last week.

JEANNE: *(Ignoring GOLDIE.)* If my son had known how to fight, he'd still be alive.

MARGARET: I agree with Goldie that we are losing our focus.

INDIRA: I don't want to take sides, but it does seem to me that we're doing exactly what the PDA warned would happen if we stopped focusing on the rules of the playground. *(Pausing.)* We're taking the same sides that our children did. *(Just then a shot rings out.)*

SHELLEY: *(Alarmed.)* What was that?

JEANNE: *(Smiling.)* Margaret lets her boys play with guns.

SHELLEY: *(Aghast.)* Real ones?

MARGARET: *(To JEANNE.)* I think it's a mistake for you to be here. You have obviously lost your focus.

SHELLEY: What happened last week?

JEANNE: *(Pleasantly.)* Margaret's two boys shot and killed my son.

SHELLEY: *(Struggling to make sense of what she is hearing.)* You mean this is some kind of game—like paintball...? Some kind of role-playing exercise... Is that what you're saying? *(There is another shot, followed by a scream. MARGARET shows some alarm. INDIRA is strangely calm.)* Oh, my God! What was *that*?

JEANNE: *(Calmly.)* It sounds like one of Margaret's boys.

MARGARET: *(Taking a breath.)* Focus.

GOLDIE: *(Confused.)* It can't be one of Margaret's boys, because they're the only ones with guns.

INDIRA: *(Smiling.)* No... Actually, my son brought a gun today.

SHELLEY: What are you talking about?

MARGARET: *(Losing her composure, she turns on INDIRA.)* You gave it to him to use against my sons!

INDIRA: He wanted a gun, and I didn't want to interfere.

GOLDIE: *(To MARGARET, gesturing with glee.)* Focus!

MARGARET: *(Regaining her composure, to GOLDIE.)* It could have been your son.

GOLDIE: *(Chin up.)* Maybe.

SHELLEY: You're all crazy. This is a game... a test or something... I'm going to look! *(She crosses to the blinds/curtains, but MADELEINE steps in front of her.)*

MADELEINE: No! We're not allowed to look out the window!

SHELLEY: Says who?

GOLDIE: It's the rules! *(SHELLEY attempts to open the blinds/curtains, but MADELEINE grapples with her. The blinds/curtains come partially open. There is another, different scream.)*

SHELLEY: That's my daughter! What are they doing to my daughter?

JEANNE: Ask Madeleine. *(MADELEINE says nothing.)* They raped her daughter last week. *(Another scream.)*

SHELLEY: Oh, my God! *(Turning toward the women.)* You're all crazy! *(She pulls away from MADELEINE and runs toward the door. MARGARET shoves a chair in front of her. SHELLEY crosses around it, but MARGARET has positioned herself in front of the door. SHELLEY stops for a moment, and then she picks up one of the chairs, as if to hit MARGARET with it. MARGARET steps to the side, and SHELLEY exits.)*

INDIRA: *(Her attention suddenly directed toward MADELEINE.)* Did you bring Christy?

MADELEINE: *(Defiant.)* No, I didn't.

INDIRA: That's not fair. We all made a commitment. *(Another shot.)*

GOLDIE: *(To INDIRA.)* What about you giving your son a gun? Now *my* son is the only boy who isn't armed!

INDIRA: It's not about gender and it's not about weapons.

MARGARET: That's right. It's about the rules of the playground.

MADELEINE: Why aren't there any safety zones for the girls?

INDIRA: It's not about gender.

MADELEINE: But girls are oppressed as a group. They're *more* oppressed! They're the most oppressed group in the school!

GOLDIE: God made boys the way they are! It's not their fault!

MADELEINE: *(To INDIRA.)* So why is it that these fancy-schmancy think tanks and peacekeeping organizations never divide the map by gender? Why don't the women of Ireland have their own country? Or the women in the Middle East? Why is it the rules of the playground never take the war against women into account?

INDIRA: You're talking like one of those 1970's feminists.

GOLDIE: It's because she's the only one of us with a daughter!

MARGARET: It's because she kept her at home! She's not really part of the program anymore. She's broken the rules.

MADELEINE: You can't answer my question! Why don't the women ever have their own base of power?

GOLDIE: *(Hysterical.)* It's the home! We already have one! We have the babies! We don't need any more power! We can negotiate with that! Every woman is her own nation! *(A round of gunshots. GOLDIE starts screaming.)* My son! My son!

MARGARET: Focus! Focus! *(INDIRA grabs GOLDIE, who is trying to see out the window. Another round of shots. GOLDIE is screaming. MARGARET turns to INDIRA.)* Close the blinds [curtains]!

INDIRA: I can't! *(More gunshots. GOLDIE breaks free and begins to run frantically between the door, which MARGARET is blocking, and the window that INDIRA is blocking. Finally, she collapses, sobbing and moaning. JEANNE watches her dispassionately for a moment, and then crosses to the windows, where she takes her time closing the blinds/curtains. She turns back to look at GOLDIE.)*

JEANNE: Goldie, I think you should have one of your brownies while we all wait for the PDA. *(Nobody moves. JEANNE picks up the brownie plate and extends it to MADELEINE.)* Madeleine, will you pass them? *(There is a long, meaningful look between MADELEINE and JEANNE. Slowly, MADELEINE crosses to the plate of brownies, and as she reaches out to take the plate from JEANNE, the lights fade.)*

Blackout

End of Play

The Boundary Trial of John Proctor

A Play in One Act

The Boundary Trial of John Proctor

A Play in One Act

The Boundary Trial of John Proctor takes up where Arthur Miller's *Crucible* leaves off. This play opens with Miller's anti-hero stumbling into the boundary lands where women's lives are lived, a territory so marginal to patriarchy that it has escaped by Proctor and his creator's awareness.

The women accused of witchcraft in Miller's play are assembled in a sewing circle. We meet Elizabeth, Proctor's pregnant wife, and Abigail, the employee he sexually exploited. We also meet Tituba, the formerly enslaved Caribbean housekeeper; Sarah, the town bag lady; Martha, the intellectual; and Rebecca, the town matriarch.

The women are assembled to make baby clothes for Elizabeth's child. They ask John Proctor to join their circle and take up the knitting. Balking at "women's work," John discovers that he is unable to assert his male supremacist values in the Boundary of women's existence. He is as marginal here as the women were in his world, and his discovery that witches are real results in an explosive verdict.

Six women, one man
Thirty minutes
Single set (bare stage)

Cast of Characters

JOHN PROCTOR: Arthur Miller's "Everyman," a 17th century, New England farmer, Elizabeth's husband and Abigail's employer. Prototypical all-American, rugged individual and self-made man. Accused of witchcraft and executed.

THE WOMEN: The women can be any age or race or ethnicity. In fact, Abigail and Elizabeth should not be the age they are in *The Crucible*. These are the characters they play:

TITUBA: A witch. An enslaved, Black woman of African Caribbean descent, executed for witchcraft.

ELIZABETH: A witch. Wife of John Proctor, mother of four children, accused of witchcraft, but received a stay-of-execution because of pregnancy.

ABIGAIL: Household servant of John Proctor, seduced by him. Prime witness at the witch trials.

REBECCA: A witch. A midwife, executed for witchcraft.

SARAH: A witch. A 17th century version of a bag lady, executed for witchcraft.

MARTHA: A witch. An intellectual, executed for witchcraft.

Scene
The Boundary.

Time
Fourth-dimensional

The Boundary Trial of John Proctor

The stage is a black box. There is only one door, upstage right. There are seven chairs placed in a semi-circle. One of them is empty. TITUBA, ELIZABETH, ABIGAIL, REBECCA, SARAH, and MARTHA are seated in the chairs. These WOMEN can be any age, any ethnicity, any race. They are busy knitting, mending, embroidering, crocheting. There is a complete silence, except for the clicking of needles. A man enters from the wings. He is JOHN PROCTOR, the middle-aged "Everyman" of Arthur Miller's Crucible. The WOMEN do not look up. Uncomfortable, JOHN does not recognize any of the WOMEN.

ELIZABETH: John...? John Proctor?

JOHN: Yes.

ELIZABETH: Come in... Sit down.

JOHN: How do you do, ladies. *(He crosses to the empty chair and sits. ELIZABETH pauses to tie off a knot on her embroidery and to rethread her needle. JOHN shifts uneasily. The WOMEN continue to work.)* I understand there is to be another trial... *(No one responds.)* I said, I'm here to be tried again. *(Again, no response.)* Look here; is this some kind of game...? What is this...? *(Silence.)* Damned if I'll sit here without knowing why. *(He gets up and crosses to the door. It's locked.)* So, that's it... I'm a prisoner. You think you have me trapped. *(He begins to pace, considering his next move.)*

ELIZABETH: *(Not looking up.)* Sit down, John.

JOHN: Oh, so somebody speaks to me. Finally. Do I get to know what I'm accused of? What do you want to hear? Adultery? I confess. Blasphemy? I confess. Perjury? I confess...

TITUBA: Do you know how to knit, John?

JOHN: *(Caught off-guard.)* No.

TITUBA: Here. *(She takes some knitting out of a bag. JOHN hesitates and then sits in the empty chair between TITUBA and ELIZABETH.)* Take the needles. *(Patiently.)* *Take* the needles, John. *(He does.)* Now, you will move all these loops to this other needle, adding a stitch each time you move one. You slide the needle under the yarn like this... *(She demonstrates.)*… and loop the yarn over, like this… *(Showing him.)* Not too tight, not too loose. And you must count, John, because this is the arm of a sweater, and you need to add stitches. Now every other stitch, you will purl, which is like this… *(Demonstrating.)* The needle goes the other way under. But careful not to miss a count or the whole pattern will be marred, and if you drop a stitch your count will be off, and you will have to rip it all out and start over. Now, knit that row, John. *(He looks around the room to see if this is a joke, but the WOMEN are deep in their work. Awkwardly, he begins to knit.)*

MARTHA: *(Not looking up.)* Now, John, start at the beginning… When Abigail first came to work for your wife.

JOHN: *(Looking up, surprised.)* I…

ELIZABETH: Keep knitting, John. Mind the count. That's three—time to purl.

JOHN: I… She came to help Elizabeth after the third boy was born.

ELIZABETH: *Purl*, John!

JOHN: Purl. She needed some help after that.

REBECCA: What was his name?

JOHN: James.

REBECCA: *(To ELIZABETH.)* I thought it was Jimmy.

ELIZABETH: It was.

JOHN: That was his nickname. Elizabeth called him that.

TITUBA: Oh, John! You weren't watching. I'll have to rip out the whole row. *(She takes his knitting and pulls out the row.)* Just pull the yarn, and the whole thing unravels. It's all just one thread.

MARTHA: I believe you were telling us about Abigail, John.

JOHN: What do you want me to say? We fornicated.

SARAH: *(Blunt.)* We're not interested in that.

JOHN: Well, it's the truth. I confess it. I confessed it to all of Salem. I'm sorry if the word offends you, but that's the name for what we did. Several times. In the barn. Yes, like animals. No, I never thought of my wife. I enjoyed it. I sinned. I confess.

SARAH: But did you call her any names?

JOHN: Yes, I called her names—"Whore," "Slut," "Bitch!" She sent a dozen people to the gallows.

SARAH: Did you call her a witch?

JOHN: A witch? *(He laughs.)* No, I never called her a witch. There's no such thing as witches. *(All the WOMEN look up at him.)* That's right. There are no witches. That's what they hanged me for. Not the adultery, not the perjury. They hanged me for the truth. There are no witches. *(He laughs again. The WOMEN just look at him.)*

TITUBA: Here. *(She hands him back the needles.)* Try it again.

JOHN: I didn't come here to knit.

MARTHA: Do you know why you came here?

JOHN: I came here for a second trial. A judgment. After they hanged me, I was sent here for a second trial.

TITUBA: *Take* the needles.

JOHN: I didn't come here to knit. I don't know how to knit. I don't want to know. I came here for a judgment.

ELIZABETH: Then you had better take the needles. We are here to judge your knitting.

JOHN: That's a joke. *(They aren't laughing.)* What does knitting have to do with the guilt or innocence of a man's soul? *(A silence.)*

SARAH: Nobody cares about your soul.

TITUBA: We are here to sew, to mend, and to knit for our families. This little sweater, John, is for your unborn child. Take the needles, or she won't have a sweater. *(JOHN takes the needles.)* Now, I have unraveled your last row. So you are starting over again. Knit one, purl one, and you want to add a stitch at the end. Do you remember how to do it?

JOHN: *(A pause.)* No.

TITUBA: Then I'll show you again. Watch. You take the needle and slide it under the stitch like this. All right? *(He nods.)*

SARAH: You were telling us about your names for Abigail—*(He starts to respond, but she cuts him off.)* Not those names... Did you call her "Abby" or "Gail?" Or your "honey bun," or your "little kitten?"

JOHN: *(Violently.)* No!

SARAH: Didn't you have a secret name for her, just between the two of you?

JOHN: No. She was just "Abigail," my wife's maid. My whore.

ABIGAIL: Are you sure?

JOHN: Yes. We had sex. We didn't talk. It was lust.

ABIGAIL: You never called her a pet name? You never called her your "little filly?" She never called you her "stallion?"

JOHN: *(Embarrassed.)* Maybe I did. I don't remember.

ELIZABETH: John, please... mind the knitting.

ABIGAIL: Abigail remembers.

JOHN: That's because she blew the whole thing out of proportion! She was crazy! She actually thought I was going to marry her, after she sent my wife to the gallows!

REBECCA: Was she pregnant?

JOHN: No. She's probably sterile.

REBECCA: How do you know?

JOHN: Because I saw her in town and in the court for about ten months after. She never got big.

REBECCA: Do you know how long it takes a woman to know she's not pregnant?

JOHN: *(Embarrassed.)* About a month.

REBECCA: Sometimes longer if she's late with her bleeding.

ABIGAIL: A month is a long time to wonder. Thirty days, thirty nights…

ELIZABETH: Do you know what happens to an unmarried woman in Salem if she's discovered to be pregnant?

JOHN: I guess they put her jail.

ABIGAIL: Thirty days to wonder about that.

REBECCA: John, did you wonder?

JOHN: Oh, I… well, I knew she wasn't. We only did it a couple of times. *(They look at him.)* Yeah, I guess I thought about it.

REBECCA: What would you have done?

JOHN: What do you want me to say? I would have done the best I could for her. I would have given her as much money as I could to help her move somewhere, some other town where they didn't know her. She could have said she was a widow.

ABIGAIL: Thirty days…

ELIZABETH: You're forgetting the sweater.

JOHN: It's hard to think of what you're doing when you have to keep counting.

MARTHA: Would you have supported her and the baby in another town, John?

JOHN: I could barely support my own family! I would have done the best I could. A man can't do more than that.

ELIZABETH: Did you support your own family?

JOHN: Of course I did. Ask Elizabeth.

MARTHA: But you died when she had three little boys and a baby on the way.

JOHN: I was hanged! That wasn't my fault! I had no choice!

ELIZABETH: *(Calmly.)* You could have confessed to witchcraft. They offered to spare your life.

JOHN: They wanted me to sign a confession—to nail it on the church door for everyone to see! A confession that I had seen the devil and that I did his work on this earth! *(He looks to the WOMEN for confirmation of his position. They are staring at him.)*

ABIGAIL: *(After a moment.)* And so you abandoned your pregnant wife and your three small children?

JOHN: I did it for them—

ABIGAIL: *(To the WOMEN.)* He said, "How can I live without my name?" *(The WOMEN burst out laughing.)*

JOHN: *(Angry.)* What's funny?

REBECCA: We all lost our names when we married.

JOHN: That's different.

ABIGAIL: Is it?

JOHN: They wanted me to *lie!* They wanted me to sign my name to a lie! *(The WOMEN exchange a smile with each other.)* Marriage is not a lie!

SARAH: John, how did you expect Elizabeth to support herself and four small children after your death?

MARTHA: Remember, as a woman, she was not allowed to inherit property, and so she wouldn't have been able to sell or lease the farm. She couldn't practice a trade, and she couldn't work the land herself with four toddlers. How did you expect her to support the family without you?

JOHN: She could have stayed with her family.

ELIZABETH: *(Watching his knitting.)* Mind what you're doing, John.

77

MARTHA: And how long would her family have been able to take care of her, with the three boys and the new infant?

JOHN: I don't know. The boys could have stayed with different families. Look, it doesn't matter. She got married again, didn't she?

ELIZABETH: But maybe she didn't want to.

JOHN: Well, then she shouldn't have married him.

TITUBA: Rip it out.

MARTHA: *(Patiently.)* Let's start over… Your wife couldn't inherit, so she couldn't sell or lease it. She couldn't work it with four—

JOHN: *(TITUBA takes the knitting away from him.)* What? *(TITUBA pulls out a row.)* I counted!

TITUBA: You've been knitting where you should have purled.

MARTHA: She would have needed to give up her children—

JOHN: What am I supposed to do?

TITUBA: Rip it out! Do it right!

ELIZABETH: You forced your wife into a sexual relationship she didn't want in order to save her children.

JOHN: Well, maybe she shouldn't have had so many children!

ELIZABETH: Refused your sexual advances…?

ABIGAIL: You forced her to prostitute herself in marriage.

JOHN: Damn it! A woman doesn't have to marry if she doesn't want to! *(TITUBA rips the knitting out of his hands again and pulls out another row.)*

ABIGAIL: So, John, if Abigail *had* been pregnant, you say you wouldn't have supported her and the baby because they weren't your family. What was *she* supposed to do?

JOHN: Do? She would go seduce some other honest, hard-working man. Oh, she could trap a man... I see what you're doing here, but it's not like you want to think it was. She was after me from the day she started working for my wife. I swear she lay in wait for me.

ABIGAIL: Was she a virgin?

JOHN: She *said* she was.

ABIGAIL: You didn't believe her?

JOHN: *(Exploding.)* I don't know if she was or she wasn't, and it doesn't matter. She was a whore. You should have seen the way she acted. She was a born whore, virgin or not.

SARAH: You didn't like the way she acted?

JOHN: Goddamit, I'm a man!

TITUBA: That's one you should have purled. You'll have to pull it out.

JOHN: Look, it's for a baby—Who cares if it has a few stitches wrong? The baby's not going to care.

TITUBA: It's all one thread. It's all one pattern, John.

JOHN: That still doesn't mean—

ELIZABETH: *(Cutting him off.)* And your wife, John...

JOHN: What about her?

ELIZABETH: What was her name?

JOHN: *(Distracted by the knitting.)* Elizabeth.

ABIGAIL: No "Betty," "Betsy," "Liza," "Libby?"

JOHN: Elizabeth. Always "Elizabeth."

ELIZABETH: Why? Wasn't she your wife?

JOHN: Just so. My wife, my mother, my judge. Saint Elizabeth.

SARAH: Was *she* a witch?

JOHN: *(A smile.)* Abigail called her one.

ELIZABETH: What about you? Did you call her one?

JOHN: There are no witches. *(Becoming angry.)* But I'll tell you what there are... There are cold women. Women who never stood a day in a man's shoes, but sit in judgment of him 'round the clock. Oh, they don't say it. They don't have to. They sit like you. Silent, smiling, superior. Bitches. That's what they are. *(He rises for a fight. They continue sewing.)*

SARAH: *(Not looking up.)* So Elizabeth wasn't a whore?

JOHN: That's a laugh! Elizabeth kept her nightgown on in bed. She wouldn't take it off—even in the summer!

SARAH: A cold woman? *(She smiles at her own joke.)*

JOHN: She was! She didn't know how to please a man. You ask her. She'll admit it. She will admit that it was her coldness that drove me to Abigail. She told me that herself. You ask her.

ABIGAIL: *(To ELIZABETH.)* Did you say that, Elizabeth?

ELIZABETH: Oh, I said that... yes. Right before he died.

JOHN: What do you mean? You're not Elizabeth! *(They all laugh except ABIGAIL.)* You don't look anything like her. *(The WOMEN laugh again.)* This woman is not my wife.

ELIZABETH: No, I'm not.

ABIGAIL: *(Still to ELIZABETH.)* Why did you say it?

ELIZABETH: I was bewitched.

JOHN: You are not my wife.

ELIZABETH: *(Losing her patience.)* I *was* your wife, John. And, look... Here's Abigail. *(He looks.)*

JOHN: No! No, that's nothing like her! Not even the right age!

ABIGAIL: What *is* the right age, John?

JOHN: Why, she was just a girl. She wouldn't even by eighteen now. And Abigail was pretty. *(The WOMEN all laugh.)* What is the matter with all of you? Are you all crazy or what? *(Silence as the WOMEN sew.)*

SARAH: *(Quietly.)* We're all witches.

JOHN: There are no witches.

SARAH: Do you know what a witch is, John?

JOHN: A woman who supposedly has traffic with the devil. A woman who does the devil's work. There is no devil, and there are no witches. *(They laugh. Suddenly he throws down the knitting.)* This is a waste of my time. I tried to humor you. I don't know what this is, but it isn't a court. It's a bunch of crazy women. *(He crosses to the door and tries to open it, but it's locked. He turns to the WOMEN.)* Open that door.

ELIZABETH: You're not ready to go out there yet. That door leads to the boundary.

JOHN: The "boundary?"

ELIZABETH: That's the place where women live. It touches your world, like the way a circle is tangent to a line, but it exists apart from it. If you are not prepared for it, John, it will annihilate you. In the boundary, the values and ways of men don't exist. You would be invisible to those who live beyond that door. As invisible as women are in your world.

JOHN: Women aren't invisible in my world. I saw more of them than I wanted to.

SARAH: What you saw were witches, John.

TITUBA: It's time to judge the knitting.

SARAH: Let's see it. *(She picks up JOHN's knitting. The WOMEN pass it around. JOHN waits by the door, uncertain how to act.)*

MARTHA: The rows are very uneven.

ABIGAIL: What few there are.

ELIZABETH: The count is off.

ABIGAIL: Way off.

REBECCA: *(Shaking her head.)* Poor…

TITUBA: Worthless. *(She rips it all out.)*

SARAH: I'm sorry, John, but your knitting has not been found acceptable.

JOHN: Good! Sentence me! Send me to prison or hang me again—and to hell with all of you!

ELIZABETH: I'm afraid you don't understand, John. You're on the Boundary here. There are no sentences, because there is no one here to do your work for you. *(She smiles sympathetically.)* You're going to have to do it over until you get it right.

JOHN: No! *(He tries to force the door.)* No! *(The WOMEN continue to knit. JOHN paces behind them. They ignore him. Suddenly, he grabs ABIGAIL by the throat, from behind.)* Open the door or she dies! *(The WOMEN look up briefly, laugh, and continue to sew.)* I mean it! *(He begins to strangle ABIGAIL. She continues to sew.)* It's impossible! She's not even choking! *(He backs away.)* She's bewitched! *(The WOMEN laugh.)* You *are* witches!

ELIZABETH: No, John, but we used to be.

REBECCA: The devil walks the earth, John. He walks the earth as sure as you're standing here. And he walks it everywhere there are men, and wherever the devil walks, the women are bewitched into worshipping him.

SARAH: Bewitched into doing things they don't want to do, pretending and believing they like it.

MARTHA: Into saying things they don't mean to achieve ends they don't want.

REBECCA: Bewitched into betraying their own sisters, their mothers, their daughters.

ELIZABETH: Bewitched into devil worship and bloody rituals involving drinking blood and eating bodies.

MARTHA: Rituals involving murderous fathers and martyred sons and virgins impregnated without their consent.

TITUBA: Bewitched into horrifying sexual initiations when they're still just girls—

SARAH: Sacrificing their bodies, killing their babies.

ABIGAIL: Women enchanted, enslaved, women asleep, women deranged, demented, destructive. Dishonest women…

ELIZABETH: Treacherous women…

MARTHA: Traitorous women…

SARAH: Sluttish women…

ABIGAIL: Bitchy women…

TITUBA: Whorish women…

SARAH: Witches, John. Every one of them.

ELIZABETH: Witches. Fantastic creatures, distorted projections.

ABIGAIL: These are the only kind of women you allow to exist in your world.

JOHN: I never wanted women to be like that. They could have been honest with me.

ABIGAIL: Abigail said she loved you.

JOHN: It was just lust. She didn't know what she was talking about. She was too young.

ELIZABETH: Your wife confronted you with your adultery.

JOHN: To judge me! She enjoyed it! It was an excuse for more of her coldness, and she admitted it herself that she drove me to it. *(There is a silence. JOHN tries to force the door open.)*

ELIZABETH: John, don't go through that door.

JOHN: What am I supposed to do?

TITUBA: The sweater isn't finished.

JOHN: And I'm supposed to feel guilty and finish it, even though I hate knitting...? You know, that's what's wrong with you women...

TITUBA: Stop talking, John.

ABIGAIL: John, we're here to help you. You can't go anywhere beyond this room unless you change the way you see things.

JOHN: You're beginning to sound like my wife after all, you sanctimonious bitch. You don't know the first thing about freedom! You belong back in Salem where they shove their moral lessons down a man's throat. Let me tell you... *nobody* tells me how to live. Nobody! I died once. I'll die again, but I'm not going to sit here and let you make a... a *woman* out of me—*(The WOMEN set their sewing down and look at each other. JOHN is actually alarmed.)* What?

ELIZABETH: Abigail, would you go and open the door for John. I think the honor belongs to you. *(ABIGAIL crosses to the door and opens it.)*

SARAH: *(Cheerfully.)* Good-bye, John.

JOHN: *(Reaching the door, he hesitates for a moment, suspecting a trick. The WOMEN are sewing. Suddenly with resolve, he crosses into the doorway.)* Good-bye! *(Awkwardly, he exits. ABIGAIL closes the door after him. She turns to face the other WOMEN. For a moment, they freeze, and then they throw down their sewing and break into spontaneous laughter. They begin to pull off their wigs and their Puritan gowns, revealing themselves to be radiant, brilliant creatures truly from another universe. They exit, arms around each other, in hysterics.)*

Blackout

End of Play

The Evil That Men Do: The Story of Thalidomide

A Radio Drama In One Act

The Evil That Men Do: The Story of Thalidomide

A Radio Drama in One Act

This one-act was originally written as a radio play, but it can also be produced as a stage drama.

The Evil That Men Do (title taken from a Shakespeare play) is the story of Dr. Frances ("Frankie") Kelsey's fight to keep thalidomide out of America. The play traces the development of her friendship with Dr. Barbara Moulton, who resigned from the FDA and was testifying against the agency's corruption at the time when Frances was hired. In her courageous act of befriending a whistle-blower, Frances was laying the foundation for her subsequent battles with the drug companies.

The play unveils the conspiracy between the German manufacturers, the American distributor, and the officials in the FDA to pressure Frances to issue a license for "the sleeping pill of the century." Frances plays for time against the good-old-boy network, while the horrifying evidence mounts that thalidomide, prescribed as a cure for morning sickness, causes severe birth defects.

Since 1960, the date of the thalidomide "scare" in this country, companies whose products are designed for women have continued to follow dangerous and deceptive practices. In 1991, a Texas jury awarded $33 million in damages to the parents of a child born with birth defects as a result of taking Bendectin, an anti-nausea drug, which had been on the market since the 1950's with *no* testing for its effect on human fetuses.

The Evil That Men Do is an old, old story—but one which points a moral for a happier ending.

Three women, eight men
Thirty minutes
Single set

Cast of Characters

DR. FRANCES KELSEY: FDA medical officer.

DR. BARBARA MOULTON: Former FDA medical officer.

DR. F. JOSEPH MORRIS: Executive assistant to Ferrell director of research.

DR. RALPH JONES: Head of the FDA New Drug Section.

DR. WILLIAM FESSENICH: Chief of the FDA Medical Division.

DR. WIDUKIND LENZ: German scientist.

FERRELL EXECUTIVE

BRUNENTHAL EXECUTIVE

BRUNENTHAL ASSISTANT

WOMAN

DOCTOR

Scene

Various locales.

Time

1960.

This play is partly a work of fiction. It is based on a true incident that did occur. However, with the exception of the names of Dr. Frances Kelsey and Dr. Barbara Moulton, the names, persons, characters, and dates have been changed and/or fictionalized

The Evil That Men Do: The Story of Thalidomide

Scene 1

WOMAN: Doctor, why won't they let me see my little girl? The nurses won't bring me my baby!

DOCTOR: I told them not to. I wanted a chance to talk with you before you saw her.

WOMAN: There's something wrong with my baby, isn't there?

Scene 2

DR. FESSENICH: Well, Ralph, today you get to meet the new medical officer in your section.

DR. JONES: You mean Dr. Kelsey? I'm looking forward to it, sir.

DR. FESSENICH: I think you'll be impressed. Dr. Kelsey has a PhD. in pharmacology as well as a medical degree. Kelsey's been in private practice for the last three years, since 1957. That should be helpful in testing and licensing new drugs.

DR. JONES: Sounds like Kelsey will fit right in. The Food and Drug Administration needs good team players. That was the problem with Barbara Moulton. She just couldn't join the team. She wasn't willing to work with anybody.

DR. FESSENICH: Well, she's quit now.

DR. JONES: Frankly, sir, I wish they all would.

DR. FESSENICH: Who?

DR. JONES: The women. A federal agency like the FDA is no place for them. They just don't understand the system.

DR. FESSENICH: Well, Ralph, I'm afraid I've got some bad news for you. Dr. Kelsey is a woman.

DR. JONES: What?

DR. FESSENICH: Dr. Frances Kelsey is a woman.

DR. JONES: But Bill... *(A knock is heard at the door.)*

DR. KELSEY: Excuse me... I'm looking for the New Drug Section.

DR. FESSENICH: You've found it.

DR. KELSEY: I'm Frances Kelsey...

DR. FESSENICH: Yes, come in Dr. Kelsey. We've been expecting you. I'm William Fessenich, chief of the Medical Division, and this is Ralph Jones, who will be your immediate supervisor.

DR. KELSEY: How do you do... Dr. Jones.

DR. JONES: Dr. Fessenich and I were discussing some of the aspects of your job.

DR. KELSEY: Oh?

DR. JONES: Licensing new drugs is high-pressure work. For some of these bigger drug companies, a week of delay can cost millions of dollars. We at the FDA have a responsibility to work within our sixty-day evaluation period.

DR. FESSENICH: Of course, if there are unusual circumstances, you can ask for an extension of this sixty-day period.

DR. JONES: That's rarely necessary. You see, Dr. Kelsey, we have a staff here of twelve chemists and twelve doctors. We get seven hundred applications for new drugs a year. We can't afford to let these cases get backed up, or we'd never license anything.

DR. KELSEY: Why are you so understaffed?

DR. FESSENICH: The FDA has never been a funding priority—and quite frankly, there's a very powerful lobby against it from the drug industry.

DR. JONES: The point is, you will be under steady pressure to meet deadlines. Now, many women who have chosen medical research have done so just to avoid this kind of pressure. My concern is...

DR. KELSEY: That I might not be able to handle the job.

DR. JONES: Well, we have recently had a woman quit the department.

DR. KELSEY: I'm sure you've had men quit, too.

DR. JONES: I think there are differences.

DR. KELSEY: I gave birth to both my daughters while I was still in medical school. I think I can handle this job.

DR. FESSENICH: Dr. Jones is just expressing a concern. It's nothing personal. I screened your application myself, and I can assure you, we've hired the best man for the job.

DR. KELSEY: Where will I be working?

DR. FESSENICH: Oh, Ralph, why don't you show Dr. Kelsey to her new office?

DR. JONES: It's down at the end of the hall, the last door on the right. I'm sure she'll have no trouble finding it.

DR. KELSEY: I'm sure I won't.

Scene 3

A soft knock is heard, followed by the sound of rustling papers.

DR. MOULTON: All right, all right... Hold your horses! I'm coming! *(The sound of a door opening.)*

DR. KELSEY: Oh, excuse me. I was looking for my office. I must have been given the wrong directions.

DR. MOULTON: No, wait... Are you Frances Kelsey?

DR. KELSEY: Yes, I am.

DR. MOULTON: Then you're in the right place. I'm just making some personal notes from these files before I leave.

DR. KELSEY: So this was your office?

DR. MOULTON: That's right. I'm Barbara Moulton, the wicked witch of the FDA. You must have been warned about me.

DR. KELSEY: No. I haven't heard your name mentioned.

DR. MOULTON: You will. I'm not planning to make a graceful exit from the FDA.

DR. KELSEY: What do you mean?

DR. MOULTON: The Senate is currently holding hearings about the FDA, and they're asking a lot of questions about the relationship between the drug industry and this agency, which is supposed to be regulating it. I'm going to testify, and when I do, I'm going to spill my guts.

DR. KELSEY: So you think there's some corruption?

DR. MOULTON: Some? It's pretty obvious you're new on the block. The FDA is here to protect the drug companies, not the consumer.

DR. KELSEY: But the new drugs have to meet certain safety criteria...

DR. MOULTON: Trust me, where there's a million, there's a way. Did you know that one of our exalted officers here has taken more than two hundred and fifty thousand dollars in private fees from drug companies to edit journals which promote the very drugs he's supposed to be licensing?

DR. KELSEY: That's hard to believe.

DR. MOULTON: You want unbelievable—how about the fact the drug companies get to distribute as many untested drugs as they want, to whomever they want, with absolutely no accountability to anyone, as long as they call it a testing program? The government has no control at all over how these companies test their drugs on the unsuspecting public.

DR. KELSEY: I'm sure the drug companies wouldn't deliberately jeopardize the health of a patient.

DR. MOULTON: Come to the Senate hearings. On second thought, you'd better not.

DR. KELSEY: Why do you say that?

DR. MOULTON: I don't think your supervisor would appreciate it. Not exactly the most positive introduction to your new job.

DR. KELSEY: I disagree. I can't think of a better orientation. And I'd like to take you out to lunch afterwards.

DR. MOULTON: Oh, that would really do it! You realize nobody in Washington will speak to me.

DR. KELSEY: I will. What about noon tomorrow?

DR. MOULTON: You sure you know what you're getting into?

DR. KELSEY: No, but I'll find out.

Scene 4

A knock on the door.

DR. JONES: Dr. Kelsey?

DR. KELSEY: Yes? Come in, Dr. Jones.

DR. JONES: Well, I see you're all settled in your new office. Not very luxurious is it? This is an old World War II army barrack.

DR. KELSEY: It's adequate.

DR. JONES: So… how do you like your job so far? Have two months been enough time for you to get used to the way we do things around here?

DR. KELSEY: I think so.

DR. JONES: Good. I have your first major assignment. It's from the William S. Ferrell Company. They're one of the oldest drug manufacturers in the country - been around for 134 years.

DR. KELSEY: Quite a shelf life.

DR. JONES: I don't mean they're not progressive. In fact this application is the first in America for a new drug that they're calling "the sleeping pill of the century." It's making quite a sensation over in Europe.

DR. KELSEY: It's already been licensed in other countries?

DR. JONES: That's right. In fact, the German manufacturer claims that already half their profits come from the sale of these pills—and they've only been on the market for three years!

DR. KELSEY: Why is it so popular?

DR. JONES: Because it puts people to sleep like a barbiturate, but it doesn't have the same unpleasant side effects. You can't die from an overdose, so people won't be able to use it to commit suicide.

DR. KELSEY: That's nice.

DR. JONES: Oh—and you should appreciate this, Dr. Kelsey… It cures morning sickness. Millions of pregnant women in Europe are enjoying their pregnancies free of unpleasant consequences.

DR. KELSEY: And what's the name of this miracle drug?

DR. JONES: Thalidomide.

Scene 5

FERRELL EXECUTIVE: Gentlemen, as representatives of Ferrell's drug testing program, you will be distributing our new little sleeping pill, Kevadon. Kevadon is our trade name for thalidomide, a drug which is currently being marketed in Germany under the name Contergan, and in England under the name Distaval. This little pill is breaking all records for sales in Europe, and we are anticipating a similar demand for the drug here in the United States. The FDA is in the process of licensing it, and Ferrell expects to release Kevadon some time in the next two months. This is where your job comes in, gentlemen. You will be responsible for making sure that the professionals in the field are already familiar with Kevadon *before* it hits the market. We want the name Kevadon to be spread among hospital staff members in every region of the country. Now, what you fellows are going to be doing, is visiting the hospitals connected with medical schools. We want you to contact the chief and senior members of the departments of surgery, medicine, and anesthesiology—and especially obstetrics and gynecology. We want you to sell these men on the benefits of Kevadon as a sedative and as a treatment for morning sickness. Leave each of these doctors with a clinical supply of pills for them to use with their patients. I want to stress to you that this program is *not* a clinical study. The safety of thalidomide has already been firmly established in laboratory tests both here and abroad. What we're doing is *confirming* what we already know about the usefulness of this drug. I cannot emphasize this point too much! Don't pressure the doctors! If they don't want to report their results—they don't have to. Tell them that we would *like* the results, and that we may send them report forms and reminder letters, but they are under absolutely no obligation to respond. Remember, we need him on our side. Try appealing to the doctor's ego. Tell him that we think he's important enough to be selected as one of the first to use Kevadon in his section of the country. Make him feel like he's part of the team.

Scene 6

Sounds of a restaurant.

DR. KELSEY: Hello, Barbara. Sorry I'm late.

DR. MOULTON: No problem. I went ahead and ordered for both of us. If you don't like your sandwich, I can eat both.

DR. KELSEY: No, it looks great. And so do you. It's been a month since I've seen you.

DR. MOULTON: I'm a new woman since I left the FDA. Speaking of which, have the drug companies started hounding you with phone calls yet?

DR. KELSEY: Not yet, but they might after this week.

DR. MOULTON: Oh? Don't tell me you're going to testify, too.

DR. KELSEY: Nothing that extreme. But I am going to turn down an application for a new drug.

DR. MOULTON: Which company?

DR. KELSEY: Ferrell.

DR. MOULTON: Oh, boy. You're in for it now. They're one of the biggies.

DR. KELSEY: I can't help it. Their data on this thalidomide drug leaves a lot of questions unanswered.

DR. MOULTON: So what else is new?

DR. KELSEY: Their studies show that the drug has a completely different effect on animals than on humans. In fact, it doesn't make animals drowsy at all.

DR. MOULTON: You must be thinking about your quinine studies?

DR. KELSEY: How do you know about those? That was twenty years ago, back when I was a graduate student.

DR. MOULTON: They were published, and I read them. Let me see if I remember... A pregnant rabbit could absorb quinine, because of the presence of a certain enzyme in her liver, but the same quinine killed her fetus, because the fetal rabbit doesn't develop that particular enzyme until after it's born.

DR. KELSEY: How could you remember that?

DR. MOULTON: Because I'm brilliant. But my brilliance aside, it's a pretty obvious conclusion. Any woman who's ever changed a baby can tell you that an infant's system is nothing like an adult's. It doesn't take a Harvard degree to figure that out. But then, these executives at Ferrell wouldn't know a baby's bottom from a hole in the ground.

DR. KELSEY: You're right.

DR. MOULTON: Of course, I'm right. If those men ever spent any time raising children they might develop a little common sense—not to mention, respect for life!

DR. KELSEY: I meant you were right that I was thinking about the quinine when I looked at the thalidomide studies. It seems to me that if thalidomide has that radically different an effect on animals, it might also have a radically different effect on human fetuses.

DR. MOULTON: So you're going to turn Ferrell down?

DR. KELSEY: I'm going to make them resubmit the application with more complete testing, and wait another sixty days.

DR. MOULTON: They're not going to like that. They've probably got their little bottles all lined up on the shelves, ready to go.

DR. KELSEY: Then they should have done it right the first time.

Scene 7

WOMAN: Doctor, what's wrong with my baby?

DOCTOR: She was born with a severe birth defect.

WOMAN: *(In a whisper.)* No.

DOCTOR: Your daughter will not be retarded. It's a physical deformity.

WOMAN: No. Bring me my baby. I want my little girl.

DOCTOR: I understand how you feel, but I think it would be better for us to talk about this before you see your baby.

Scene 8

A knock on the door.

DR. MORRIS: Dr. Frances Kelsey?

DR. KELSEY: Yes? Come in.

DR. MORRIS: Allow me to introduce myself. I'm Dr. Joseph Morris, executive assistant to the Ferrell director of research.

DR. KELSEY: Oh, yes. I remember your name on the new data on thalidomide that you sent last week.

DR. MORRIS: Yes. We were, of course, impressed by your thoroughness in evaluating the initial application—and more than happy to send you the additional data you requested…

DR. KELSEY: You didn't send the data I requested.

DR. MORRIS: Please, Dr. Kelsey, allow me to finish. We at Ferrell, as I said, are impressed with your thoroughness, and I assure you it will be an asset in licensing *new drugs*—but in this case, it's not applicable, because Kevadon has been in on the market overseas for three years, since 1957. And in those three years, there have been no reports of problems. Kevadon is currently being sold in twelve countries in Europe, seven in Africa, seventeen in Asia, and eleven here in the Western Hemisphere. It's already been licensed in Canada. So you can see that the kind of research you're requesting has obviously been done, and the drug is obviously safe.

DR. KELSEY: If the tests have already been done, then I'm sure your company won't mind sending the results to my office.

DR. MORRIS: That's not the point, Dr. Kelsey.

DR. KELSEY: What is the point, Dr. Morris?

DR. MORRIS: The point is that we are in production and ready to market Kevadon. My company is unwilling to wait another sixty days for a second evaluation of data that has already been proven unnecessary.

DR. KELSEY: Dr. Morris—It's my job to evaluate data on new drugs before they are licensed for sale and distribution in this country. That is what I have been hired and trained to do. That is my job. It is my professional opinion that Ferrell's data on thalidomide is inadequate to warrant FDA licensing, and until your testing can meet my criteria, I will not approve the drug.

DR. MORRIS: *(Switching tactics.)* You've only been with the FDA for five months, haven't you?

DR. KELSEY: That's right.

DR. MORRIS: And how do you like living in Washington?

DR. KELSEY: I enjoy it.

DR. MORRIS: And your family?

DR. KELSEY: They enjoy it, too.

DR. MORRIS: Big change from the Midwest, isn't it?

DR. KELSEY: In some ways.

DR. MORRIS: I understand you were in private practice there in South Dakota—a country doctor, weren't you?

DR. KELSEY: You seem to know a lot about me.

DR. MORRIS: We like to know the medical officers who handle our applications. It's a good neighbor policy. You must know about that from your practice.

DR. KELSEY: I practiced as a doctor, not a neighbor.

DR. MORRIS: Well, Mrs. Kelsey...

DR. KELSEY: Doctor.

DR. MORRIS: Doctor. I know that out in the country there's a lot of distance between farms—there's a real need for some give and take between folks...

DR. KELSEY: Dr. Morris, I have a lot of work to do...

DR. MORRIS: What I'm getting at is that, for all it's red tape and regulations and bureaucracy, when you come right down to it, the government in Washington isn't run all that different from those farms out in South Dakota. When a man needs a roof on his barn, his neighbors come over to give him a hand, because they know that when it's time for their barn to get a new roof, they can count on him to help them out.

DR. KELSEY: The FDA is an independent federal agency.

DR. MORRIS: The FDA is people, Dr. Kelsey, people just like those barn builders in South Dakota, people just like you and me. And when you need that extra data and another sixty days on a new drug, we'll bend over backwards to see that you get it. We will. But when we have a perfectly safe drug on our hands, like Kevadon, we expect you'll bend a little bit to help us get it on the market and out to those people who need it. That's just good neighbors and good sense, isn't it?

DR. KELSEY: This study you submitted is not the data I requested. You will have another sixty days to resubmit. And now, Dr. Morris, if you'll excuse me, I'm very busy.

DR. MORRIS: Certainly. Perhaps your supervisor won't be quite as busy. *(The sound of a door closing.)*

Scene 9

A phone rings.

DR. JONES: Hello... This is Dr. Jones... Yes... Yes... Well, Dr. Morris, I understand your impatience, but Dr. Kelsey is highly qualified. I'm sure that when she finishes her evaluation of the data... What's that? Oh... She has. Well, then what's the problem? The wording on the label? Well, if it's only a question of haggling over a word or two, I don't see why you couldn't settle that over the phone. I see... I see... And did Dr. Kelsey know that Ferrell is all ready to start printing the labels? And she still wouldn't return your phone calls? No, Dr. Morris, I can't think of any explanation for her behavior, especially since, as you say, she's already approved the drug... Well, she's new on our staff. This is her first assignment. Yes, I know, but the FDA is just people, Dr. Morris. Of course. And I will speak with her. Yes... Yes...Fine. You call me if you have any more problems. *(He slams down the phone receiver.)* Women.

Scene 10

DR. KELSEY: Well, Barbara, they did it.

DR. MOULTON: What did they do, Frankie?

DR. KELSEY: Just what you said they would. They tried to go over my head.

DR. MOULTON: Right on schedule. Who did they talk to?

DR. KELSEY: My supervisor, Dr. Jones. Morris called him and told him that I had already approved thalidomide, and the only question left was about the wording on the label.

DR. MOULTON: Yep. That's the way they do it.

DR. KELSEY: He complained that I wasn't returning his phone calls.

DR. MOULTON: Shame on you.

DR. KELSEY: And I'm sure the two of them had a nice conversation about my erratic female behavior.

DR. MOULTON: I'm sure.

DR. KELSEY: Why should I return a phone call, when I have nothing new to report?

DR. MOULTON: Why indeed.

DR. KELSEY: And can you imagine Morris telling Jones that I had approved thalidomide?

DR. MOULTON: Yes.

DR. KELSEY: That was a bald face lie.

DR. MOULTON: Well, Frankie… Now you know why I quit.

DR. KELSEY: I know. You warned me. But it's still hard to believe when it happens to you.

DR. MOULTON: So what are you going to do?

DR. KELSEY: I'm going to make them submit the application a third time and wait another sixty days.

DR. MOULTON: I don't think you'll get the votes for "Most Popular Girl."

DR. KELSEY: How about "Most Likely To Succeed?"

DR. MOULTON: We'll see.

Scene 11

BRUNENTHAL EXECUTIVE: I knew it! I knew it! This is exactly what I predicted would happen!

BRUNENTHAL ASSISTANT: What is that, sir? Is our company in trouble again?

BRUNENTHAL EXECUTIVE: I told those distributors in England it would be a mistake, and now, it's just as I predicted! The American distributors are starting to ask questions.

BRUNENTHAL ASSISTANT: Is it thalidomide again, sir?

BRUNENTHAL EXECUTIVE: There is nothing wrong with thalidomide. Nothing!

BRUNENTHAL ASSISTANT: But in England they kept getting those reports…

BRUNENTHAL EXECUTIVE: Those reports! Those reports! Don't you think Brunenthal gets reports, too? Look here! *(He opens a file drawer.)* Four hundred of them. Don't talk to me about reports.

BRUNENTHAL ASSISTANT: You mean there have been cases in Germany of polyneuritis?

BRUNENTHAL EXECUTIVE: Polyneuritis! The big words. You tell me what polyneuritis is.

BRUNENTHAL ASSISTANT: Well, sir, I thought it was a case of nerve damage...

BRUNENTHAL EXECUTIVE: Exactly! Nerve damage! You tell me what kind of nerve damage!

BRUNENTHAL ASSISTANT: Well, sir, I understood that it made people go numb in the arms and legs, and then they couldn't walk, and sometimes they get double vision and can't see, and sometimes they can't talk, and it makes their face twitch and their whole body tremble...

BRUNENTHAL EXECUTIVE: Nerve damage! Let me ask you something. What is thalidomide?

BRUNENTHAL ASSISTANT: A sleeping pill, sir?

BRUNENTHAL EXECUTIVE: Exactly! A sleeping pill! And what kinds of people take sleeping pills?

BRUNENTHAL ASSISTANT: Uh... people who can't sleep?

BRUNENTHAL EXECUTIVE: Exactly! People *who can't sleep*! People with *bad nerves*. So what kinds of problems are they going to report? Nerve problems. You see? Now, the British, when they got these reports, they panicked. They started to print warnings on the labels. But at Brunenthal, we didn't panic. We investigated. We took our pills to a place where people are not such hypochondriacs.

BRUNENTHAL ASSISTANT: Where was that, sir?

BRUNENTHAL EXECUTIVE: The public mental asylums. You see? And guess what? No more stories about nerve problems. Poof. Gone.

BRUNENTHAL ASSISTANT: But most people in mental asylums can't report on their condition.

BRUNENTHAL EXECUTIVE: People are people! Statistics are statistics. Our studies show that this so-called nerve damage is very, very rare and completely reversible as soon as the patient stops taking the pills.

BRUNENTHAL ASSISTANT: But in England, they found the damage was permanent in twenty percent of the cases.

BRUNENTHAL EXECUTIVE: In England, in England! The doctors in England—who knows where they get their reports? Maybe they need a German company to blame for their own malpractice. Who knows?

BRUNENTHAL ASSISTANT: So what are we going to tell Ferrell when they ask about the reports of polyneuritis?

BRUNENTHAL EXECUTIVE: We tell them the truth: Thalidomide is perfectly safe.

BRUNENTHAL ASSISTANT: But what about the four hundred cases reported here in Germany?

BRUNENTHAL EXECUTIVE: I told you! Those four hundred cases are misleading. It would be irresponsible to share these reports with Ferrell, because it would create an unhealthy prejudice in their minds.

BRUNENTHAL ASSISTANT: So you're not going to mention them at all?

BRUNENTHAL EXECUTIVE: I thought we might want to select a few of the more accurate ones… Thirty-four is a nice number. Yes, we will tell them we have had thirty-four cases.

BRUNENTHAL ASSISTANT: Is that honest?

BRUNENTHAL EXECUTIVE: Honesty and truth are two different things, my boy. The truth here is that thalidomide is safe and millions of people are benefiting from it. We don't want to sacrifice the truth just for the sake of a little honesty, do we? We can't let ourselves lose sight of the woods for the trees!

Scene 12

DR. MORRIS: Knock-knock. *(Sound of a door opening.)*

DR. KELSEY: Dr. Morris, you need to make an appointment…

DR. MORRIS: Not necessary. Just dropped by to remind you, in case you forgot.

DR. KELSEY: Forgot what?

DR. MORRIS: That March 6 is our date to release Kevadon for marketing. Wasn't that what we agreed on?

DR. KELSEY: I don't recall that we've agreed on anything.

DR. MORRIS: Perhaps it was your supervisor, then.

DR. KELSEY: Then you can talk to him. Have you seen this, Dr. Morris?

DR. MORRIS: What is it?

DR. KELSEY: A copy of the *British Medical Journal* from last December. There's a letter in it from a doctor in Scotland: "Is Thalidomide To Blame?"

DR. MORRIS: Let me see.

DR. KELSEY: He reports four cases of polyneuritis in patients who were taking the drug. The nerve damage has not reversed itself, although they stopped taking thalidomide months ago. Does your company know about these reports?

DR. MORRIS: I seem to remember something like this.

DR. KELSEY: Why weren't reports of this sent to me, Dr. Morris?

DR. MORRIS: Nervous symptoms of this nature are not really relevant to the application process...

DR. KELSEY: "Nervous symptoms?" Doctor, some of these patients can't walk and can't see anymore, and apparently the damage is permanent. You don't think this information is relevant to the licensing of thalidomide?

DR. MORRIS: It's a factor in using the drug, certainly, but you didn't let me finish. The British distributer is adding a warning to the label, and we at Ferrell are prepared to take the same precaution. At the point where the FDA is ready to talk about the wording on the label, that would have been the appropriate time to discuss these reports.

DR. KELSEY: That would not have been the appropriate time. Dr. Morris, I want your company to get me a complete list of all the doctors to whom your company has distributed samples of Kevadon for human experiments.

DR. MORRIS: *(Alarmed.)* What would you do with a list like that?

DR. KELSEY: I plan to find out just how many American users of thalidomide have developed these "nervous symptoms."

DR. MORRIS: But we have a March 6 release date!

DR. KELSEY: Then you'd better hurry.

DR. MORRIS: Don't patronize me, Dr. Kelsey. You know as well as I do that many barbiturates on the market have toxic side effects. Frankly, Dr. Kelsey, I think you should know that your unreasonable behavior has raised some pretty serious questions within your own agency about your competency.

DR. KELSEY: I agree this case has raised many serious questions about competency. I am considering your application withdrawn. You will have to resubmit with the data I requested for another sixty-day period.

DR. MORRIS: But March 6…

DR. KELSEY: Good-bye, Dr. Morris.

Scene 13

A phone rings.

DR. JONES: Hello, New Drug Section… Dr. Jones speaking. *(A pause.)* Who is this…? Oh, Dr. Morris. Yes? *(A pause.)* Doctor, you'll have to slow down. I can't understand a word. Now, what is this you want to read to me…? A letter from Dr. Kelsey to your company. This must be about the thalidomide licensing. Go on. *(A long pause.)* Yes… Yes… She says your studies are inadequate… *(A pause.)* And there were cases of nerve damage in England that your company knew about but didn't disclose… So? *(A pause.)* Libel? I don't know that I'd characterize the letter as libel. Doesn't that seem a little extreme…? Oh… Your lawyers don't think so. *(A pause.)* Yes, a lawsuit would certainly be very unpleasant for Dr. Kelsey… Well, she is the medical officer who was assigned to study your application. Unless she resigns or asks to be removed from the case, I can't really justify reassigning it to someone else… *(A pause.)* What? What about the letter…? You want me to reconsider it? It's on FDA letterhead, isn't it? Unless you can give me sufficient reason, I don't see how I can reconsider it. *(A pause.)* All right. All right. I'll talk to her, but I can't promise you anything… Fine. If you want to talk to the chief of the Medical

Division, you go right ahead. *(He slams down the phone receiver.)* Women!

Scene 14

DR. FESSENICH: Come in, Dr. Kelsey. Please sit down. I believe you know everybody here.

DR. KELSEY: I believe I do, Dr. Fessenich. Dr. Jones... Dr. Morris.

DR. FESSENICH: I've called you all together this afternoon, because over the last eight months, there seems to have been a lot of misunderstanding about this Kevadon business. I thought if we could all sit down in a room together and talk this thing over, we might be able to find out just what the problem is and how to straighten it out. Dr. Morris...

DR. MORRIS: Our position is one, frankly, of frustration. We have submitted four applications—four volumes of data, each one the size of a Manhattan phone directory. Each time we submit, we are told to wait sixty days. At the end of those sixty days, we are told to submit again. Kevadon is hardly an experimental drug. It's been on the market now for three years in other countries, and out of the millions of users, only a handful react with minor and reversible nervous symptoms...

DR. KELSEY: They can't walk and they can't see.

DR. MORRIS: Please let me finish, Dr. Kelsey. You gentlemen can see what I'm up against.

DR. KELSEY: You are up against the FDA.

DR. MORRIS: Dr. Fessenich, would you like me to finish speaking?

DR. FESSENICH: Please. Dr. Kelsey, we'll hear your side in a minute.

DR. MORRIS: There seems to be no professional justification for these delays—and there seems to be no end in sight. Dr. Kelsey's methodology defies our researchers. Ferrell is willing to do whatever is required to obtain the license, but it is impossible for us to determine what exactly this is, because Dr. Kelsey wants something different every week.

DR. FESSENICH: Dr. Kelsey?

DR. KELSEY: Ferrell has still not submitted the data I requested eight months ago.

DR. FESSENICH: And what data is that?

DR. MORRIS: Who knows?

DR. KELSEY: Studies which show that thalidomide will not harm the fetus in a pregnant woman.

DR. MORRIS: Pregnant women for years have been taking the drug safely. Thousands of them.

DR. KELSEY: I have not received any fetal studies.

DR. FESSENICH: Is there a particular reason why you need this type of study?

DR. KELSEY: There's always a need to study the effects on a fetus. In this case, we already know thalidomide can damage adult nerve tissue, which is relatively tough. There's a strong possibility it can also damage fetal tissue, which is very delicate, especially in the first months of pregnancy.

DR. MORRIS: This was your particular area of graduate studies, wasn't it?

DR. KELSEY: If Ferrell spent as much time researching thalidomide as they have apparently put into researching my life, this meeting might not have been necessary.

DR. JONES: Dr. Morris was only pointing out what's natural to all of us. Every researcher has his—or her—area of specialization, and it's only human nature to put an emphasis on that area where we feel most competent. I believe that's all that Dr. Morris was trying to get at. Perhaps your interest in fetal testing is a case in point. I would also suspect you have a vested interest, having been a mother.

DR. KELSEY: Then you must have a vested interest too, having been a fetus.

DR. FESSENICH: Dr. Kelsey, would you be satisfied if Ferrell could provide you with studies on pregnant women?

DR. KELSEY: Yes.

DR. FESSENICH: And would you be willing to provide these studies, Dr. Morris?

DR. MORRIS: If that's what Dr. Kelsey has decided she wants, that's what she'll get.

DR. FESSENICH: Well then, that seems to be the solution. Are you sure that this will satisfy you, Dr. Kelsey?

DR. KELSEY: As long as the data is conclusive.

DR. MORRIS: Don't worry—it will be.

Scene 15

WOMAN: Doctor, how badly deformed is my baby?

DOCTOR: It's pretty severe.

WOMAN: *(Quietly.)* Tell me... what she looks like.

DOCTOR: Her arms are stunted. She has no elbows. In fact, the hands seem to grow right out of the shoulders.

WOMAN: Is... there more?

DOCTOR: She has no legs.

WOMAN: Oh, God.

DOCTOR: Do you want me to go on?

WOMAN: What else is there?

DOCTOR: Her face.

Scene 16

FERRELL EXECUTIVE: So, Morris, how was your meeting over at the FDA? Did we get the Kevadon license?

DR. MORRIS: Not yet, sir.

FERRELL EXECUTIVE: Damn that woman!

DR. MORRIS: But we did get Kelsey to say she would be satisfied if we could produce data showing thalidomide was safe for fetuses.

FERRELL EXECUTIVE: Has anyone here done a study like that?

DR. MORRIS: Not that I know of.

FERRELL EXECUTIVE: Then let's get our director of Medical Research to write one. We can get it published in the *American Journal of Obstetrics and Gynecology.*

DR. MORRIS: But won't it look bad if it's done by one of our people?

FERRELL EXECUTIVE: I just said he'd *write* it. We can always find some other doctor in the field to let us use his name to publish. Those guys love to see their names in print.

DR. MORRIS: We should try to use a doctor who has been distributing samples of Kevadon to his patients.

FERRELL EXECUTIVE: That's right. And we'll say he phoned his reports in. That way there won't be any written records.

DR. MORRIS: Do you have someone in mind, sir?

FERRELL EXECUTIVE: There's a Ray Nelson in Ohio. He'd do it for us.

DR. MORRIS: Is he an obstetrician?

FERRELL EXECUTIVE: No, but I don't think that matters. If the article is in the obstetrics journal, people will just assume he is.

DR. MORRIS: How soon can we get this?

FERRELL EXECUTIVE: What's today... May 10? I think we can get it out in the June issue.

DR. MORRIS: I'd like to see Kelsey wiggle out of this one.

Scene 17

Sounds of children playing in a park.

DR. MOULTON: So you want to know what I think of a so-called independent study which just happens to appear right at the exact moment when Ferrell needed one?

DR. KELSEY: Barbara, I already know what you think.

DR. MOULTON: What do *you* think?

DR. KELSEY: I think, even if the study is legitimate—which there's no way of proving without a Senate investigation, it still doesn't prove anything. The Nelson study is about women who took the drug during the last three months of their pregnancies. It's the first three months I'm worried about. That's when the fetus is most sensitive. That's the data I need.

DR. MOULTON:
So you're going to make them resubmit for the fifth time?

DR. KELSEY: I'll have to.

DR. MOULTON: You realize no one's going to be in your corner this time, don't you—not even the FDA?

DR. KELSEY: What about you, Barbara?

DR. MOULTON: Oh, you know me. I'm always on your side.

DR. KELSEY: Then they're hopelessly outnumbered.

Scene 18

Sound of a door opening.

DR. MORRIS: Dr. Kelsey…

DR. KELSEY: No.

DR. MORRIS: May I come in?

DR. KELSEY: No.

DR. MORRIS: Ferrell is going to put Kevadon on the market before Christmas. This means we'll need to print labels next month, in early October. You and I need to talk about what these labels are going to say.

DR. KELSEY: No.

DR. MORRIS: If this isn't a convenient time, why don't I call and give you the labeling changes over the phone?

DR. KELSEY: No.

DR. MORRIS: So you're not even going to discuss this, are you?

DR. KELSEY: No.

DR. MORRIS: That seems kind of narrow-minded for a scientist, don't you think?

DR. KELSEY: No.

DR. MORRIS: A lot of people are starting to talk about your strange behavior, Dr. Kelsey. Did you know that?

DR. KELSEY: No.

DR. MORRIS: I'll call you next week... and maybe you'll feel more like talking then.

DR. KELSEY: No. *(He slams the door.)*

Scene 19

WOMAN: Doctor, why? Why is my baby deformed?

DOCTOR: We don't know the cause.

WOMAN: Is it my fault?

DOCTOR: I can't say.

WOMAN: I quit smoking. I tried to watch my weight. Is it because I kept my job? I didn't think that would hurt the baby... Other women work when they're pregnant...

DOCTOR: I don't know what caused it.

WOMAN: Why don't you? You're the doctor. You're supposed to know. *(Crying.)* Why did this happen to my baby?

Scene 20

BRUNENTHAL EXECUTIVE: Dr. Lenz?

DR. LENZ: Yes?

BRUNENTHAL EXECUTIVE: May I come in?

DR. LENZ: Who are you? What do you want?

BRUNENTHAL EXECUTIVE: I represent Brunenthal, the company that manufactures thalidomide. These two men are my assistants. We would like to talk to you about your studies.

DR. LENZ: *(Wary.)* Come in.

BRUNENTHAL EXECUTIVE: Thank you. Nice home, Dr. Lenz. You must be a very successful scientist.

DR. LENZ: I enjoy my work.

BRUNENTHAL EXECUTIVE: Your work. Why don't you tell us a little bit about your work?

DR. LENZ: Why don't you tell me why you're here?

BRUNENTHAL EXECUTIVE: We are concerned about this theory of yours that thalidomide is causing birth defects.

DR. LENZ: It's no theory. I can prove that every one of the mothers of deformed babies in my studies took thalidomide during her pregnancy.

BRUNENTHAL EXECUTIVE: Birth defects have been around a lot longer than our drug, Dr. Lenz.

DR. LENZ: Not this particular kind, with the hands growing out from the shoulders like flippers. It's very, very rare. At least until two years ago. Now there's an epidemic here in Germany. Just last month, September, there were twenty-seven cases in Kiel.

BRUNENTHAL EXECUTIVE: I read the newspapers, too. I also read that everybody has a different theory. This one says it's a detergent. This one says it's radioactivity in the air. This one says it's a new virus. Everybody wants to be a hero.

DR. LENZ: The only thing these women have in common, other than this tragic experience, is that each one took thalidomide during her pregnancy.

BRUNENTHAL EXECUTIVE: Oh, come now, Doctor. They all *say* they took it, but do they really remember? These are pregnant women we're talking about. Maybe they bought some sleeping pills, but do they really remember which brand? Or maybe their doctor gave them some pills, but did they really remember to take them? Maybe they want to be helpful to the important doctor. Maybe they want to find someone else to blame...

DR. LENZ: My studies are all based on hospital records, not the testimony of the subjects.

BRUNENTHAL EXECUTIVE: My company would like to see these studies.

DR. LENZ: I'm going to publish them.

BRUNENTHAL EXECUTIVE: We would like to see them before they're published.

DR. LENZ: Why?

BRUNENTHAL EXECUTIVE: So that we can verify that what you say is true.

DR. LENZ: You don't plan to withdraw your drug, do you?

BRUNENTHAL EXECUTIVE: Not without a good reason. May we have your original data, please?

DR. LENZ: I am keeping the originals.

BRUNENTHAL EXECUTIVE: Maybe you want to keep them, because they aren't the truth?

DR. LENZ: Maybe you want to have them, because they are.

BRUNENTHAL EXECUTIVE: *(Turning nasty.)* If you publish these studies, Dr. Lenz, we are prepared to sue.

DR. LENZ: More publicity.

BRUNENTHAL EXECUTIVE: Publicity? Right now we are preparing a brochure, "Thalidomide Is A Safe Drug." We are printing 70,000 copies, and we will distribute these all over Europe. You won't get away with this, Dr. Lenz. We will do everything we can to stop you. You are murdering an innocent drug!

Scene 21

A knock on the door.

DR. MORRIS: Dr. Kelsey... May I talk to you?

DR. KELSEY: Dr. Morris, there is no reason for you to continue to harass me. I have nothing new to say to you. You have threatened me with lawsuits, hounded me with phone calls, and turned my supervisors against me. You have done your worst, and I am not given in, and I will not give in...

DR. MORRIS: *(He interrupts her.)* Doctor, I'm here to apologize. *(A pause.)* Thalidomide has just been taken off the market in Germany.

DR. KELSEY: Oh? "Nervous symptoms?"

DR. MORRIS: No, actually... *(He clears his throat.)* It seems there were some reports of birth defects.

DR. KELSEY: Birth defects!

DR. MORRIS: Terrible, of course, if it turns out to be true, but Brunenthal insists that these cases are just coincidences.

DR. KELSEY: So the German government had to take it off the market?

DR. MORRIS: Yes... Ferrell is still hoping that there is some other cause for these...

DR. KELSEY: Dr. Morris, you need to contact every doctor in this country who has been distributing test samples of these drugs to their patients. They must be notified immediately! To think it was used to treat morning sickness! Thank God there were no more than sixty doctors in America with your testing program.

DR. MORRIS: Sixty? Where did you get that idea?

DR. KELSEY: From you... You mean there are more?

DR. MORRIS: Well, actually, there are... twelve hundred.

DR. KELSEY: Your company gave an unlicensed drug to twelve hundred doctors, with instructions to hand them out to their patients? That's unbelievable! And how many pills have you given out?

DR. MORRIS: Mmmm... I believe about... two and a half million.

DR. KELSEY: Oh, my God... Dr. Morris, we have to contact all of these doctors and pick up these supplies immediately. They have to warn their patients.

DR. MORRIS: But shouldn't we wait to see whether it's a coincidence?

DR. KELSEY: On second thought, I want you to send me the names and addresses of these doctors. I'll have FDA agents contact them. And I need these immediately.

DR. MORRIS: I suppose this means you'll want Ferrell to resubmit the application?

DR. KELSEY: Dr. Morris, I consider your application permanently withdrawn!

Scene 22

A phone rings.

DR. JONES: Hello... Jones, here. Oh, yes, Morris... Of course I know about the Senate hearings... Of course, Kelsey's going to testify. I don't know what she's going to say! How would I know...? No, I'm not going to talk to her. You talk to her... Why the hell not? You've called her every week for the last twelve months about that damned license...! Well, get off my back then. I can't help how your company is going to look. You found out about the birth defects back in November. You were still trying to distribute it experimentally until March. Now how the hell are you going to

114

explain that? That's your problem... You want to talk to Kelsey, you call her! *(He slams down the phone receiver.)* Kevadon!

Scene 23

A bottle of champagne is opened.

DR. MOULTON: Congratulations, Dr. Frankie! Here's to the winner of the President's Award for Distinguished Civilian Service! *(She clinks.)*

DR. KELSEY: And here's to the woman who blew the first whistle! *(She clinks.)*

DR. MOULTON: I noticed there wasn't anyone from the FDA at your award ceremony.

DR. KELSEY: I didn't invite them.

DR. MOULTON: *(Laughing.)* I'll bet they're furious that you've been appointed to head the new division for testing experimental drugs.

DR. KELSEY: I'm just glad Congress finally did something about regulating those drugs. If Kevadon had had to be licensed before Ferrell passed it out to those doctors for testing, it never would have left the laboratory. And those nine babies would never have been born without arms and legs.

DR. MOULTON: True, but at least it was nine instead of ten thousand, like they had over in Europe.

DR. KELSEY: None of this should have ever happened anywhere. One birth defect is too many.

DR. MOULTON: I'm just glad you were at the FDA when that application came through. Anybody else would have licensed it a year ago.

DR. KELSEY: I didn't do it alone. If you hadn't already been through a witch-hunt, I wouldn't have known what to expect, and I wouldn't have been able to take such a strong position. You deserve the award as much as I do.

DR. MOULTON: You know who really deserves the award?

DR. KELSEY: Who?

DR. MOULTON: The mothers. The mothers who took thalidomide.

End of Play

A Labor Play

A Play in One Act

A Labor Play

A Play in One Act

A Labor Play is a satirical piece about what might happen if surrogate mothers become a commodity in the corporate world. The two chief executive officers are concerned about the bad publicity that might result from a worker's desire to gain control over the distribution of the goods. (The mother has decided to keep the baby.)

The collision of male dominance with the women's value system is violent, and the scenario, in light of the "Baby M" case, might not be as far-fetched as it seems.

One woman, two men
Fifteen minutes
Single set

Cast of Characters

FRANK: the male CEO of a corporation, played by a woman

JOE: a male junior executive, played by a woman.

MARY: a teenaged woman.

SECURITY GUARD: a male, played by a woman.

Scene

The interior of the office of a corporate CEO.

Time

The present.

A Labor Play

The scene is in the office of the chief executive of a large manufacturing firm. FRANK sits behind his desk. He is reviewing the terms of a labor contract. JOE enters. FRANK and JOE are played by women.

FRANK: *(Rising.)* Joe. *(He extends his hand.)*

JOE: *(Extending his hand.)* Frank. *(They shake hands, hitch their pants, sit, lean back, and sigh in unison.)*

FRANK: Now... what's all this business about a strike?

JOE: Well, that's what it is, sir.

FRANK: Fire them all. They're not in a union.

JOE: Well, I'm afraid that's going to cause some pretty unpleasant publicity. You see, the public hasn't completely adjusted to the idea of...

FRANK: Right, right. I spoke too soon. You're absolutely right. This isn't meatpacking, is it? We've got to move a little slower... Give the man on the street a little time to catch up to the new technology. *(He pauses, walks to the window.)* Joe, we're on the brink of a whole revolution in industry. We, you and I, are in the vanguard of that revolution. Our company and its product are going to change the way the world lives... the way it eats, the way it worships, the way it fights. We are going to change every single aspect of life in the twenty-first century. Right now it just seems like a small innovation, but in the next five years, when we begin our phase of corporate expansion, especially when we begin to set up branches overseas, we are going to turn the world upside down and inside out. This industry is going to set America back on course. This industry is going to stem the tide of deficits to other countries. This industry is going to bring the world to America's doorstep. We are the future. But there's a lot of old-fashioned customs we're going to have to work around before we gain acceptance. We've got to move slowly. Now, what do the strikers want?

JOE: Well, really, there's just one troublemaker. The rest are just showing their solidarity.

FRANK: Good. Good. And what does their leader want?

JOE: Well, you're not going to like this, sir. There's clearly a Marxist influence at work in this. The workers say they want control over the manufactured goods... specifically; they want to control the distribution.

FRANK: *(A grave expression.)* That's to be expected... at least for a while, until the public begins to understand the vital importance of this business to the community. We've got to move slowly until we have the government on our side. Of course, they already are, but they still have to be responsive to public opinion. Well, normally, I'd say fire the worker, but I think in this case we may have to make some concessions. Has the press got hold of this yet?

JOE: No, sir.

FRANK: That's a surprise.

JOE: Well, sir, I think the workers are a little embarrassed about contacting them, because of their part. You see...

FRANK: *(Cutting him off.)* Oh, yes. Well, naturally they might be. Good. Good! That works to our advantage. Now, have you offered some compensation in salary... maybe more benefits... say, some extended maternity leave?

JOE: I suggested that we might be open for negotiating, but the workers... Well, sir, they seem to think it's a question of... *(He looks down and coughs.)*... love.

FRANK: *(Stunned for a moment. Neither man looks at each other.)* Love. Yes. Well, I suppose we might have anticipated this too. I'm a little new at all this, coming from Hormel. You'd never hear a striker there talk about their love of chili. *(He laughs. JOE doesn't.)* Of course, that was meatpacking. Not the same.

JOE: *(Soberly.)* Not the same at all, sir.

FRANK: Well... so... It's love, is it? And how much is this "love" going to cost us?

JOE: That's just it, sir. They say there's nothing to negotiate about.

FRANK: Nothing to negotiate! There's always something to negotiate. Why would they strike if they didn't want something? Come on, Joe! You weren't born yesterday. Of course they'll negotiate. They're holding out for something.

JOE: *(Looking at his shoes.)* They want to keep the... product.

FRANK: Well, they can't. That's company property. We have a contract.

JOE: They say they made it, so it's theirs.

FRANK: Hogwash. We hired their labor, paid for the components, leased the facilities. Go ask their leader what she wants. *(He indicates that JOE should do it now. JOE takes a few steps towards the door, and then suddenly he stops.)*

JOE: *(Turning to face FRANK.)* She wants the baby.

(Just then the door bangs open. MARY, a very young and very angry woman, stands in the entrance, taking in the scene for a few seconds. She strides to FRANK's desk and throws down a wad of bills.)

MARY: There. There's all the money you paid me for my food, rent, utilities, doctor bills... for the last nine months. All of it. Every cent. I've changed my mind. I'm keeping my baby.

FRANK: Miss...

MARY: Never mind my name. Just count the money. Then I'm going. I'm going to take my baby home.

FRANK: *(He exchanges a look with JOE. JOE gets the message and slides out the door.)* Well, now, Miss... my friend... There's no need for me to count the money. I'm sure it's all there...

MARY: With interest.

FRANK: ... with interest. But you see, that isn't the point. Now, please sit down. *(She doesn't.)* Please. I want us to understand each other. *(She sits.)* What if an assembly-line worker at the Ford Motor Company decided to quit? Would he... *or*, she... be able to plunk down nine months' salary and demand the removal of all the windshields he or she had fitted in those nine months?

MARY: This isn't a windshield. It's a baby. My baby.

FRANK: Well, yes. I understand the difference.

MARY: Good. I'm the mother, and it's mine.

FRANK: Wait a minute there. Hold your horses, Miss… my young friend. We have a legal agreement, you and I. A contract. *(He produces it.)* You built that baby with nutrients supplied by our company. You assembled that baby in a space leased by us. Your work was supervised and inspected by our doctors. We own that baby, my friend. We are the parents.

MARY: I didn't build it… It grew by itself. You didn't lease my uterus. You can't do that. It's mine. And if I was desperate enough to sign some lousy piece of paper, that still doesn't mean you could lease it. People can't sell their bodies.

FRANK: *(Smiling.)* You women have been doing that for centuries.

MARY: No! You men are just selfish and vain enough to believe you could buy them.

FRANK: I'm not here to argue. The fact is you are an adult, and you signed that contract of your own free will.

MARY: My own free will! Ha! Since when have I had my own free will? I'll tell you about my own free will! I was raised with movies about waiting for Prince Charming. I played with Barbie dolls. I grew up with magazines for girls that sold more space for ads than they did for articles. Ads which told me to have softer skin, moister lips, silkier hair, bigger breasts, smoother thighs, higher heels, lower necklines, and a scented vagina. I read books about patient and loving women who waited hand and foot on unreasonable men, and were rewarded with his undying gratitude and love, and a castle or two in England. I learned in church that I had to be humble and obedient. I learned in school about the history of great men and the books of great men. At home, I learned my place. And when I found a boy who said he loved me… a boy who asked me to prove I loved him, where had I ever been taught that this wasn't my destiny? Where had I ever been taught to say "no?" Where had I ever been taught that I had a right to a body which all my life I had been grooming for this very moment? And then when I got pregnant, and he told me I was trying to trap him, where did I have any practice with showing anger? Where had I ever learned that this might have been someone else's fault and not mine? Hadn't I teased him with my appearance, hadn't I let it happen, hadn't I neglected to use birth control, and hadn't I wanted to make him stick around because of the baby? It's all true. And because I live in a state that has cut off the funds for abortions, I couldn't afford one. And that too was my fault. I'm poor. I can only make seventy-six cents to the dollar that men make. Like half the women I know, I've had to change jobs twice because of sexual harassment. I can't afford a nice wardrobe for the better secretarial jobs. I have to have a uniform job, so I work as a waitress. I make less than minimum wage and depend on tips, but men still think they're being generous to leave anything for me. I'm supposed to be flattered and grateful for my honest day's wage. I don't even get to believe I earned it. And still this is all my fault. And since I can't get an abortion, I have to have the baby. So I read your ads for mothers who can't afford their babies...

FRANK: Our ad states "Women who want to put their babies up for adoption."

MARY: It's the same thing.

FRANK: Not at all.

MARY: To most of us, it is. Anyway, I couldn't support myself through the pregnancy, because at the restaurant where I work, I'm supposed to look sexy and wear a short skirt and a low-cut blouse, and so, of course, after I started to show, I knew I would be fired, because pregnancy spoils the illusion. Sex isn't sexy when you connect it with babies. And I don't have a car, or a phone, because I can't afford one, and I knew that I wouldn't get a job after I started showing, because everybody would assume that I was going to quit work after it came, although I don't know what they thought I would live on. And, yes, I wanted the baby to be healthy. So, I answered your ad, and I signed your contract. But I did not sign it of my own free will. I have never had my own free will, at least until now. And I want my baby.

FRANK: Well, I'm sorry, because you're not going to have it. It belongs to the company. Whoever's fault it is, you signed away your rights. The courts will uphold our contract. In fact, they already have.

MARY: The courts are wrong.

FRANK: *(Smiling.)* The courts are the law.

MARY: The courts are men's law.

FRANK: Always the victim, aren't you? *(MARY gets up and moves towards the door. Just then, JOE appears in the doorway. He blocks her exit.)*

MARY: Get out of my way.

JOE: *(Restraining her.)* Where are you going?

MARY: To get my baby.

JOE: You won't find it in the nursery.

MARY: What do you mean? *(She stops struggling.)*

JOE: *(Letting go of her arms.)* We have removed it to a special security area.

MARY: *Where?*

JOE: I'm afraid I can't tell you that.

MARY: *(Turning to FRANK.)* Where? *(FRANK just smiles kindly at her. She rushes towards his desk and lunges for him. JOE restrains her, as FRANK steps into the hall and summons the SECURITY GUARD, a male role also played by a woman. At the sight of the GUARD who is armed, MARY stops struggling.)*

FRANK: The security guard will escort you off the premises. *(He goes to the desk and picks up the wad of bills and extends it towards her.)* I suggest that you take your wages. You have earned them. There's no reason not to take them. And we might be able to arrange some termination pay... *(She spits in his face. FRANK turns abruptly and puts the money back in a drawer in his desk. MARY is led out of the room. JOE stays. There is a moment of silence after her removal.)* Get an injunction to keep her off the property—no publicity, of course. I think we should find a buyer for her unit as quickly as possible.

JOE: No problem. We've got more orders than we can fill.

FRANK: Good. What's the current market price?

JOE: Twenty thousand through a private attorney. Higher on the black market, depending, of course, on the color.

FRANK: Well, let's say twenty thousand for now. We can review that figure again before Christmas. *(JOE starts to leave.)* Oh, Joe... Do you have kids?

JOE: *(Surprised, he turns.)* Uh, two, sir.

FRANK: Well, I hope that doesn't affect your ability to make responsible decisions.

JOE: I have always made it a policy to keep my family life separate from my work.

FRANK: Good. Good. *(JOE turns to leave again.)* Girls?

JOE: One of them.

FRANK: *(Pleasantly.)* And how old is she?

JOE: *(Turning back.)* Sixteen.

FRANK: Really? Well, we might be able to find some work for her...

JOE: *(Embarrassed.)* Thank you, sir, but she's got other plans.

FRANK: *(Laughing.)* Well, don't they all? Keep it in mind. It's a good offer. Might pay her college tuition.

JOE: *(Uncomfortable.)* Thank you, sir.

FRANK: Good job, Joe. Here's a little bonus for your trouble. *(He opens the drawer, and extends the wad of bills. JOE does not approach to take the money. To avoid a confrontation over it, FRANK crosses to him and places the money in his hand.)* Here, now, you've earned it. Get a little something for the kids.

JOE: *(Taking the money, he once more starts to leave, but turns back to ask a question.)* Sir?

FRANK: Yes?

JOE: Do you have any children?

FRANK: This… *(Thumping the desk.)*… is my baby.

Blackout

End of Play

Heterosexuals Anonymous

A Recovery Meeting in One Act

Heterosexuals Anonymous

A Recovery Meeting in One Act

Five women come together for a regular meeting of Heterosexuals Anonymous, an organization designed to help women overcome their unmanageable addictions to men. The women share their experiences of automatically deferring to men, of battering, of rape, of sex discrimination, and of inability to relate to the males in their own families.

The women, having admitted that they were powerless over their addiction to men, work through the steps of the program towards recovery. The steps include Step Two: "Believing that a power greater than men can restore us to sanity" and Step Four: "Making a searching and fearless moral inventory of all the men in our lives, including fathers, brothers, husbands, and sons."

A lighthearted spoof, the play nevertheless points up the political analysis which is lacking in tradition 12-Step programs, a lack which often leads women to believe personal growth is possible without social change.

Five women
Twenty minutes
Single set

Cast of Characters

PEGGY: A woman in her 40's or 50's.

LOU: A fat woman.

KAREN: A woman wearing a business suit.

SHIRLEY: A new member to the meeting, in her 30's.

KARONDA: An exotic dancer.

Scene

A meeting room for Heterosexuals Anonymous in the town where the play is being presented.

Time

The present.

Heterosexuals Anonymous

A meeting room for local Twelve-Step programs. The members of Heterosexuals Anonymous—PEGGY, LOU, KAREN, and KARONDA—arrive and begin setting up chairs in a circle for the meeting. There may be a literature table that one of the members is stocking with pamphlets. There may also be a refreshment table, with coffee and cookies. The members may or may not greet each other. If they do, the ad-libbing should be minimal. This is an established weekly meeting and the members have been attending for many years. The setting-up procedures are routine, almost mechanical. When the chairs have been set up, the women take their seats. SHIRLEY enters tentatively.

SHIRLEY: Heterosexuals Anonymous?

KARONDA: That's us.

LOU: Welcome. *(SHIRLEY takes a seat cautiously.)*

PEGGY: *(Checking her watch.)* Well, I guess we can get started... Welcome to the [name of town where play is being presented] open meeting of Heterosexuals Anonymous. I'm Peggy. I'm a recovering heterosexual.

ALL: Hi, Peggy.

PEGGY: I'm chairing tonight's meeting. I've asked Karonda to read the Twelve Steps.

KARONDA: Hi. I'm Karonda, and I'm a recovering heterosexual.

ALL: Hi, Karonda.

KARONDA: *(Reading from a book.)* "These are the steps we have taken:

One: We admitted we were powerless over our addiction to men, and that our lives had become unmanageable.

Two: Came to believe that a power greater than men could restore us to sanity.

Three: Made a decision to turn our will and our lives over to working for women, *as we understand them.*

132

Four: Made a searching and fearless moral inventory of all the men in our lives, including fathers, brothers, husbands, and sons.

Five: Admitted to ourselves and to other women the exact nature of these men's wrongs.

Six: Were entirely ready to remove these defective characters from our lives.

Seven: Humbly asked other women to help us remove these men.

Eight: Made a list of all the men who had harmed us, and became willing to confront them all. We also made a list of all women we had betrayed, neglected, and withheld support from, and became willing to make amends to them all.

Nine: Confronted directly, whenever possible, the men who had harmed us, and demanded reparation, except when to do so would endanger ourselves or another woman. We also made direct amends to the women we had harmed, except when to do so would require turning our resources over to men.

Ten: Continued to take inventory of men and when they were wrong, to promptly confront them.

Eleven: Sought through radical action to raise the consciousness of women, *as we understand them*, working only for what will benefit ourselves.

Twelve: Having had a feminist awakening as the result of these steps, we tried to carry this message to heterosexual women and to practice these principles in all our affairs."

PEGGY: Thank you, Karonda. I'd like to ask us to pause for a few moments of silence to reflect on why we are here. *(Moment of silence.)* Is there anyone here who has been free of men for less than thirty days?

SHIRLEY: *(Raising her hand.)* I'm Shirley, and I'm just visiting tonight.

ALL: Hi, Shirley.

PEGGY: Hi. I'm still Peggy, and I'm still a recovering heterosexual.

ALL: Hi, Peggy.

PEGGY: I was thinking about a topic for tonight, and I came up with "deference," because even though I have been free of men for twenty years, I still find myself tempted to defer to them. I was raised in a family where my younger brother got all the attention, because he was a boy. I learned to clean up after him, and to give him the last of the cookies, and to protect him whenever he was in trouble, even though he was always telling on me. I loved music, and I learned to play piano by ear, but it was my brother who got the lessons and joined the band at school. I was a model girl—quiet and modest, and I was very flattered when my boss began to date me when I was just nineteen. My brother, of course, had gone to college, but I had to work. Anyway, I was a typist in an insurance company, and the owner of the company had just been divorced and he began to ask me out. I was, of course, flattered. He was much older than I was and he seemed to have so much power. And then he asked me to marry him. It never occurred to me to say no. I had never said no to a man in my life. I didn't know how—so I married him, and I soon realized that it was like my brother all over again, except that this man had children he hadn't told me about, and now I had to take care of three people instead of one. He had told me that he would send me to college, but somehow that never happened. I had a nervous breakdown the second year of the marriage. I was twenty-one. I wanted to go back home, but my mother told me that I was a grown woman now, and that I couldn't run away from my responsibilities. So I went back. And I began to drink. My life was a wreck. My husband found that I was more of a burden than a helper, and he stopped being nice to me. I ran off with a man I met in a bar. I was so starved for affection. He left me, and I began to sleep with a lot of different men. I was drinking a lot. But one thing I did was, I signed up for a music appreciation course at a community college. And my teacher was a wonderful woman. She didn't take any shit off the men in the class. I was really drawn to her. One day I went to her office to ask her about other music classes, and I found myself just crying and crying. She had all these wonderful pictures of famous women musicians around her office. I never even knew there were any. I told her how much I admired her, but that I felt that my life was ruined, because of the drinking. She said it sounded like the real problem was the heterosexuality. This was a surprise to me. I had never heard such an idea in my life, but it struck a deep chord of truth in me, and I asked her about it. She said that she had been "male-identified," which was another word I had never heard, but that she had gotten herself in a program and turned her life around. I asked her what program she meant, and she told me about Heterosexuals Anonymous. I had never even known there was such a thing. I went to a meeting, and right from the first meeting, I knew this was where I belonged. I got myself clear and over it, and I began to meet and cultivate friendships with some wonderful, strong, self-directed women who shared the same interests that

I did. I went back to school full-time, working in the music library at the university, and now I have my own all-women jazz band. I owe my life to Heterosexuals Anonymous. Now, I'd like to open up the meeting. Would anyone like to share any thoughts on tonight's topic, deference?

KAREN: I'm Karen, and I'm a recovering heterosexual.

ALL: Hi, Karen.

KAREN: Thank you for your story, Peggy. I work in a real estate office where I train and supervise fifteen agents—most of them men. I have been in recovery for five years, and I know what Peggy means when she says the temptation to defer to men hangs around for a long time. Last week, this new guy joined the office, and he was being introduced to me. He was one of those men we in HA call a "charmer." *(Murmurs of assent.)* I was shaking his hand, and he said, "It's certainly going to be a pleasure to have such a good-looking boss." And I was so shocked I didn't know what to say. The other men in the office were watching to see what I would do, and the first thing I thought was, "Don't be rude." This was what we call the "Curtsey Reflex." And I fell for it. I smiled at him and said, "Thank you." And he smiled and walked off, and I had that terrible feeling that we all know so well of having given away my power to a man. And the whole office had watched me do it. I realize I should have asked him what he meant – you know, turned it around and put him on the spot. Sometimes I feel that old pull for their approval, and I just have a hard time turning it around on them. The conditioning is just so deep, and they know just how to use it. I'm grateful for HA, where I have been able to hear other women and how they turn it around and take their power back. I would never have risen to a management position without HA.

PEGGY: Thank you for sharing.

KARONDA: I'm Karonda, and I'm still a recovering heterosexual.

ALL: Hi, Karonda.

KARONDA: I really hear what Karen said. I work as an exotic dancer, and because I am always surrounded by men, I think I stay pretty much on top of my addiction. A lot of women in recovery wonder how I can do it—you know, dancing on tables for drunk men, but let's be real—I can make a hundred dollars a night for a few hours of dancing. It's not like I have to fuck them or anything, you know? It's my way of turning it around, you know. And in my business, I see men in their natural state as predators, so it's easy for me to stay clear and over it. But every now and then, when all the guys are trying to cop a feel when they put the money in my bra, or when they're yelling obscenities at me—every now and then, there will be this guy who seems embarrassed. And he says he's here with his buddy, and he had no idea what kind of place this was, and he apologizes for his friend's rude behavior. And then he asks me how I feel about working there. You know, not a "charmer," but one of those so-called Genuine Nice Guys. And I have to catch myself. I start thinking, "Wow, look! Here's one who's actually all right. Maybe I could take him up on a drink. It couldn't hurt to have a conversation with him." You know how it goes—don't want to hurt his feelings or anything. *(Murmurs of assent from the others.)* And here's the best—I really caught myself thinking this!—"Those women in HA are just men-haters…" *(Laughter.)* "… They think all women should be just like them. Some men are really trying, and if we don't take the time to reward these guys, they'll just end up as bad as the rest." *(Understanding nods.)* The old "Nanny Reflex." I've been in recovery for eight years, and I still have to catch myself. If it wasn't for these meetings, I don't know what I'd do. Probably I'd be fucking them again—you know, hating myself.

LOU: I'm still Lou, and I'm still a recovering heterosexual.

ALL: Hi, Lou.

LOU: I want to say that HA has saved my life. When I came to my first meeting, I was scared to death. I thought, "These are all just men-hating dykes, and they're all just trying to make converts." *(Laughter.)* I remember I was scared someone was going to try to pick me up. *(Pausing, she laughs.)* I wish! *(Laughter.)* But when I came to my first meeting, I had a black eye and a broken nose. I guess I knew that the next time I would die. I had been doing men for a long time. I never knew there was anything else. I had been molested by my father when I was a child, and then I was date-raped in high school—only I didn't know that' what it was. I had an abortion. Actually, I've had three. And then I got with Joey. And I figured I was so bad that I was lucky to have a man at all. *(The women shake their heads in sympathy.)* And the women at work, they were all addicted to men, only they didn't know it, and I just thought that was the way women were. They would see the bruises and the black eyes, and they would just pretend not to notice. In fact, they would get kind of nervous—artificially cheerful—like this was some kind of reflection on them, which of course it was. Well, anyway, I saw how they acted, and I just figured the battering must be my fault. Joey was calling me "fat bitch" and stuff like that all the time—and because I was heterosexual, I thought that being fat meant I was ugly… *(Murmurs of sympathy.)*… and I figured it was painful for him to be with such an ugly woman. So I thought when he beat me, it showed that he cared. Anyway, I was getting pretty "numbed out." I was in the third stage of men addiction. I was thinking about killing myself, stuff like that. And then this girlfriend of mine who used to know me in high school—Well, she had gotten clear and over it, and she came by to visit, and it was right after a really bad episode of battering. I looked pretty bad, and she was real concerned. And I said all the usual things: "Oh, it's getting better, really." Or, "I said some things that I knew would really punch his buttons. He's right, I really can be a bitch." But she didn't buy it. I kept trying to laugh it off and get her talking about her boyfriend, but she just kept wanting to hear about everything—when it started, what else he had done, names he called me—everything. I was surprised how much denial I had been in. She was really making me look at it. I had never met a recovered heterosexual. All the women I knew were practicing their addiction. And she told me about HA. And at first I just couldn't get over the lesbian thing. I just got this terrible revulsion thinking about women doing it to other women. But she said to me, "Lou, this guy comes home, beats you up, and then he rapes you while he's insulting you and threatening you... Come on—you can't get any kinkier than that!" So I thought, "Well, yeah." So we went to a meeting and I thought, "Yep. Dykes – every one of them..." *(Laughter.)* And I figured they didn't have any fun and they all hated themselves—all the myths that heterosexuals have to rationalize their behavior. But there was something there—I couldn't really name it, but it kept me coming back. And it was that these women weren't lying to each other anymore, because they had stopped lying to themselves. Anyway, I come to every meeting I can. It really does work. *(There is a moment of silence.)*

PEGGY: I'm Peggy and I'm a recovering heterosexual.

ALL: Hi, Peggy.

PEGGY: We have some more time, and I thought of something that happened to me a few weeks ago. I had the flu and stayed home from work for three days. I got tired of reading, and I watched television. *(Murmurs of concern.)* I knew I shouldn't, but I thought, "Well, I'm sick—what's so bad about it?" And of course the soap operas were on, and I was watching all of these women taking their boyfriends so seriously and obsessing on them—and I got kind of caught up in the stories, like I would have before I came to consciousness and got over it. And then the ads where all the women are either infantile or else they're all in leotards, twenty-one, and weigh a hundred pounds. And after the first hour, I stopped being insulted and angry. I just started to numb out on all the color and movement. I know I should have just turned it off, but I didn't. It's a reminder that I need to keep working my program and coming to meetings. I've been woman-identified for twenty years, and I was completely hypnotized after an hour. *(There is another period of silence.)*

SHIRLEY: Well, since everyone else has spoken, I guess it's my turn to speak. I'm Shirley, and I'm a heterosexual.

ALL: Hi, Shirley.

SHIRLEY: This is my first meeting... and... I have a three-year old son. *(She breaks down in tears. The others wait in silence.)*... and... I look at him and I think he's just a child, and he needs me. But then I feel like I can't stand it anymore. He acts just like his father, and his little male friends all run around with guns, and they talk to me already like they haven't got any respect... and I... I can't hate my own child—I just can't! *(She is crying again. KARONDA puts a hand on her shoulder.)*

KARONDA: First things first, honey.

SHIRLEY: Do I come ahead of my son?

KARONDA: It's a selfish program.

KAREN: I'm still Karen, and I'm still a recovering heterosexual.

ALL: Hi, Karen.

KAREN: We don't cross talk in HA, but I had a son also. If you are a heterosexual woman, there is no such thing as healthy sharing with males. I had to get to that first step and admit that my life was unmanageable. I was convinced that my boy child would be different. A lot of heterosexual women believe that. But I was unable to stand against all his friends, his teachers, what he saw on TV, how he saw other mothers with their sons and husbands, and my own poisonous conditioning. I could not control his access to my resources. I had to put my recovery first, and I gave his father custody when we divorced. And it was hard. The only support I had was these HA meetings. When you are addicted to men, you are in a system that supports it, and lots of times these people you think love you are not happy to see you get healthy. They are sick themselves. That's why they're with heterosexual women. So... I took it one day at a time, and I have been clear and over it for five years. It's still a struggle. Nobody says it's going to be easy. But it is going to be worth it. *(PEGGY looks at her watch.)*

PEGGY: Well, I think it's time to close. Are there any burning desires to speak? *(Silence.)* Okay, let's join hands for the Sorority Prayer. *(The women stand and join hands. PEGGY recites the prayer.)* "Give me the serenity to accept the women who cannot be changed, / The courage to help the women who can, / And the wisdom to know the difference."

ALL: Keep coming out—*It works!*

Blackout

End of Play

The P.E. Teacher

A Play in One Act

The P.E. Teacher

A Play in One Act

The P.E. Teacher is a suspenseful thriller exploring the interface of misogyny, racism, and homophobia in the public schools.

Dana Willets, an African American lesbian, has just been hired to teach P.E. classes at Rosa Parks Middle School. She is replacing another lesbian teacher who resigned suddenly in mid-term under mysterious circumstances. Dana's attempts to discover the reason for this resignation are frustrated by the vice principal, who lectures her on the need to be a team player.

Dana recognizes the English teacher Anne, who is white, as a former lover from college, and as she presses her for information about the P.E. teacher, Anne becomes increasingly nervous and uncommunicative. An African American girl is assaulted in the halls by male students, and the school nurse, guidance counselor, and vice principal engage in a cover-up of the incident, focusing their attention on the attitude of the victim.

As information about the P.E. teacher's resignation begins to surface, Anne is scapegoated for her recent breakdown, and a gun that was concealed in the sofa of the lounge resurfaces in the violent resolution of the drama.

Five women, one man, two girls
Thirty minutes
Single set

Cast of Characters

(Casting by age and race is open unless otherwise specified)

DANA WILLETTS: The new PE teacher, an African American woman, mid-thirties.

VICTORIA: The vice principal.

RUDY EINHORN: The computer teacher, a gay man.

AMANDA JENKINS: The guidance counselor.

JOAN: A white girl, twelve years old.

SERENA: An African American girl, twelve years old.

NURSE: The school nurse, a white woman.

ANNE: The English teacher, a woman in her mid-thirties.

Scene
The interior of the teachers' lounge at Rosa Parks Middle School.

Time
1997.

THE P.E. TEACHER

Lights come up on a teachers' lounge in a middle school. It's 1997. There are tables and chairs, a couch, a refrigerator, and a counter with cabinets, a telephone, a microwave, a hot plate, and an electric coffee-maker. In front of the couch is a coffee table with magazines. There is a row of windows across the back of the lounge. The environment is sterile. The teachers' lounge is empty. The door to the lounge opens slowly and ANNE enters. ANNE, 35, is an English teacher. She dresses conservatively and her movements are furtive. She is carrying something wrapped in a sweater. Crossing to the sofa, she lifts one of the cushions and places an object underneath it. Hearing noises in the hall, she leaves quickly. A moment later, DANA and VICTORIA enter. DANA, an African American woman, is in her mid-thirties. DANA, a physical education teacher, wears comfortable, sporty clothes. She is a lesbian, and she does not make any effort to disguise the fact. VICTORIA, a woman also in her mid-thirties, is aggressively dressed for success. She wears clothing appropriate for a corporate executive.

VICTORIA: *(Showing DANA around.)*
And last, but not least—the teachers' lounge. An island of sanity in an ocean of chaos. There's usually coffee on, but by this time of day, drink at your own risk. No smoking, of course. And there's a microwave, and the refrigerator... *(Opening the refrigerator door.)* If you leave food in here, be sure to put your name on it, and whatever you don't eat during the week gets thrown out on Friday. And this concludes our tour of Rosa Parks Middle School. Do you have any questions?

DANA: *(Smiling.)* When do I start?

VICTORIA: *(Checking her watch.)* In about a half hour. We're having an all-school rally for the big game this weekend, and I thought that would be the most appropriate place to introduce the new P.E. teacher to the students.

DANA: And the "big game" is...

VICTORIA: The annual football game between the Rosa Parks Panthers and the Rivercrest Rattlesnakes.

DANA: Sounds more like a high school athletic program than a middle school.

VICTORIA: It's our most successful after-school program—

DANA: For the girls?

VICTORIA: For the boys. And the games are very well attended. We've had good response from the parents. *(DANA doesn't respond.)* Would you like some coffee?

DANA: *(Watching her.)* No, thank you.

VICTORIA: *(Pouring herself some coffee.)* So what do you think of our school so far?

DANA: I'm looking forward to coaching the girls' teams.

VICTORIA: You don't think they'll be intimidated by a teacher who's played professionally?

DANA: I hope they are.

VICTORIA: Oh?

DANA: I want them to take the game seriously.

VICTORIA: Doesn't that sound more like a high school athletic program than a middle school?

DANA: *(Smiling.)* You don't have to have a big game in order to take a sport seriously. You just need to have good role models.

VICTORIA: *(Returning the smile.)* Like yourself?

DANA: I think so.

VICTORIA: And what makes a good role model?

DANA: A teacher who never tells a girl that her dreams are unrealistic.

VICTORIA: *(Smiling.)* Even if they are?

DANA: That's what all my teachers told me, and I made it.

VICTORIA: You might have been the exception.

DANA: Every girl might be an exception. The exceptions just might be the rule.

VICTORIA: Quite a motivational speech. I hope the girls appreciate your zeal on their behalf.

DANA: They better.

VICTORIA: I have to tell you, Dana, I had certain reservations about hiring someone so overqualified for the job. If you don't mind my asking, why didn't you take a job coaching at a university?

DANA: Because this is the age when the right teacher can make a difference. This is the age when girls get lost.

VICTORIA: Oh, I think you can find plenty of lost girls at college.

DANA: Maybe, but the fourteen-year old girl who's pregnant and drops out of school is probably not going to get back in the game.

VICTORIA: Maybe she defines the game differently than you. Maybe her game *is* marriage and a family.

DANA: Maybe, but I'm going to show her there's another way to live.

VICTORIA: Dana, your idealism is admirable, but I want to warn you that this is a very small community, and it's one with its own culture and rules. You might do well to keep a low profile until you can "learn the game," so to speak. Feminism doesn't play too well in Peoria. *(Just then she sits on the corner of the sofa where the gun is stashed.)* Oh! *(Spilling her coffee.)* What is this? There's... something... under here. *(Pulling out the gun.)* A gun!

DANA: Let me see... *(Taking the gun.)* Ruger .357 Magnum six-shot revolver. Nice. *(Checking.)* Loaded.

VICTORIA: *(Looking under the other cushions.)* What was it doing in the sofa?

DANA: Maybe one of the teachers left it here...?

VICTORIA: Teachers aren't allowed to bring weapons to school.

DANA: Lots of women carry guns like this in their purses these days.

VICTORIA: Well, they shouldn't. *(DANA looks at her.)* They might be taken and used against them.

DANA: You don't really believe that, do you? *(VICTORIA looks at her sharply.)* What about soldiers? Don't they know that they could get captured and have their weapons used against them? Maybe we should take all their guns away, too?

VICTORIA: We're not talking about a war.

DANA: We aren't?

VICTORIA: *(Ignoring her remark.)* And a gun certainly doesn't belong in the sofa of the Teachers' Lounge. *(She puts it in a cabinet.)*

DANA: *(Watching her.)* Victoria, I do have a question about the school. *(VICTORIA turns.)* Why did the PE teacher leave in the middle of the term?

VICTORIA: She resigned.

DANA: Why?

VICTORIA: *(Turning to clean up the spilled coffee.)* It seems she didn't have good boundaries with her students. It was her decision to resign.

DANA: What do you mean by "good boundaries?"

VICTORIA: She developed an inappropriate relationship.

DANA: How was it inappropriate?

VICTORIA: Is persistence one of the qualities of a good role model? *(DANA waits.)* Barbara was a lesbian. *(DANA waits.)* We don't have any prejudice against gay teachers here. In fact, we have several on faculty, but we can't protect a teacher if she chooses to make an issue of it.

DANA: What exactly did she do?

VICTORIA: *(Looking squarely at DANA and smiling.)* She resigned. *(VICTORIA turns to refill her coffee cup. Just then RUDY and AMANDA enter. They are engaged in a rapid and lively conversation. AMANDA is the school guidance counselor. Bubbly and flirtatious, she wears expensive, but trendy clothes. RUDY, the math and computer teacher, wears a sports jacket and tie. Officially in the closet, everybody on faculty knows RUDY is gay.)*

AMANDA: *(Laughing, with an arm on RUDY's shoulder.)* No!

RUDY: ... and *then, Jory*—

AMANDA: Not Jory!

RUDY: ... *Jory* tells me that it wasn't his idea. He says it was *Jeff*—

AMANDA: Of course, of course. And I'm sure Jeff said it was someone else's—

RUDY: Oh, you *know* they weren't going to admit who it was!

AMANDA: Oh, of course.

RUDY: But I wasn't going to react—

AMANDA: That's what they wanted, to get a rise out of you.

RUDY: So to speak.

AMANDA: *(Swatting him.)* Oh, you're bad!

RUDY: So I had Jory give a report to the class on his latest discoveries on the Internet.

AMANDA: You didn't!

RUDY: I did. He was *totally* embarrassed—

AMANDA: Well, I guess so. You know how boys are at that age.

RUDY: Tell me about it—I *was* one!

VICTORIA: *(Crossing toward them.)* Rudy, Amanda... I'd like you to meet our new PE teacher. Amanda Jenkins, this is Dana Willetts... Dana, Amanda, our school guidance counselor. And Rudy, this is Dana. Dana, Rudy Einhorn, the math and computer teacher.

RUDY: *(Extending his hand.)* Dana—welcome to Rosa Parks.

VICTORIA: *(A hand on DANA's shoulder.)* If you'll excuse me, I need to make sure they announce the assembly before the bell. *(She exits.)*

RUDY: So, you're taking over for Barbara?

DANA: That's right.

AMANDA: Well, I know the girls will be relieved. They've had practically a different sub for every class.

RUDY: I understand you played for the San Jose Lasers.

DANA: That's right.

RUDY: Pretty impressive. Our biggest athlete before you was the history teacher who won the six kilometer at the Founder's Day Race.

AMANDA: And never let us forget it.

RUDY: Must have been tough to leave the Lasers.

DANA: *(Smiling.)* It was time.

RUDY: So what brought you all the way from San Jose to Rosa Parks?

DANA: This was the first school willing to hire me with my qualifications.

AMANDA: Aren't you certified?

DANA: I mean my *over*-qualifications.

AMANDA: Oh.

RUDY: Well, I'd say we got a deal.

DANA: So did I. I'm looking forward to the challenge.

RUDY: These kids are challenging.

AMANDA: Rudy was just telling me how his boys discovered pornography on the Internet this morning.

RUDY: Had to happen. Just glad they didn't have to learn about it from some Radio Shack clone out in a dark alley somewhere.

147

AMANDA: Well, I think you handled it just right.

DANA: And how was that?

AMANDA: He didn't react.

RUDY: I asked the ringleader to give us a report on what he had found.

DANA: And what about the girls?

RUDY: Oh, they weren't involved.

DANA: It's a boys' class?

RUDY: Oh, no, there were girls in the class, but it was the boys who were causing all the trouble. The girls weren't interested.

DANA: And they weren't upset?

AMANDA: Oh, heavens! It's not like they haven't seen pornography. The boys are always trying to bring *Playboy* to school, taping up the pictures in their lockers. The girls have learned to ignore it.

DANA: *(To RUDY.)* You don't think some of them were upset?

RUDY: I don't think they saw enough of it to have any reaction. The boys were just surfing through the websites—

DANA: My point is that it might have been an opportunity to explain that pornography is hate speech and that it isn't a joke to the women and girls whose lives are impact—

RUDY: Whoa, whoa, whoa… Who says it's hate speech?

DANA: Who says it isn't?

AMANDA: Well, there are lots of women who are uncomfortable with it, but who don't feel that censorship is the answer.

DANA: They don't know what they're talking about.

AMANDA: That sounds a little presumptuous.

DANA: They don't. The women who talk about the First Amendment haven't the faintest idea of what hard-core pornography is about. Have you ever seen it?

AMANDA: Oh, certainly—

DANA: *(Cutting her off.)* "Babyrapers-dot-com?" "www.pussywhip—

RUDY: *(Fleeing.)* If you ladies will excuse me...

AMANDA: *(Confused.)* Oh. You're going?

RUDY: Grading papers... Nice meeting you, Dana. *(He exits quickly.)*

AMANDA: Bye.

DANA: Well?

AMANDA: What?

DANA: Pornography. Have you seen the hard-core stuff?

AMANDA: I guess I haven't. And I think this conversation drove Rudy off.

DANA: That's too bad, because it sounded like he could use some input on the subject.

AMANDA: Have you had lunch?

DANA: No. If he's got boys using class time to report on pornography, what kind of message is that going to send the girls?

AMANDA: *(Her back to DANA.)* Oh... Someone has put something in here that's spilled all over everything! I don't know why people can't be more careful. And they put these open, half-empty soda cans in here— which are just going to go flat anyway – and they never come back and finish them, and then they get spilled... *(Getting paper towels.)* What a mess! *(DANA realizes that AMANDA is cutting her off. She crosses to the cabinet and takes out the gun.)*

DANA: Is this your gun?

AMANDA: *(Not turning.)* What?

149

DANA: Your *gun*? *(AMANDA turns. She reacts with fear to the sight of DANA holding a gun.)* Someone left it in the teachers' lounge.

AMANDA: No. I don't know anything about guns. I've never owned one.

DANA: Ruger .357 Magnum six-shot revolver. A good gun for a woman to have.

AMANDA: I prefer to resolve my conflicts a little less violently.

DANA: A gun can produce a remarkably calming effect.

AMANDA: Well, guns make me nervous. I wish you'd put it away. *(There is a knock on the door.)* Excuse me. *(She crosses to the door and opens it. JOAN, a twelve-year-old, white girl, stands in the doorway.)*

JOAN: Uh… is Miss Carter here?

AMANDA: No, she's not.

JOAN: Do you know where she is?

AMANDA: I think the vice principal has gone to her office. *(JOAN starts to leave.)* Can I help you with something? *(The girl confers with someone on the other side of the door.)*

JOAN: Do you know when she'll be back?

AMANDA: Is there something wrong?

JOAN: My friend, she fell down the stairs, because the boys were trying to pull up her dress—

AMANDA: Who fell?

JOAN: *(Turning to the side.)* Serena. *(She pulls SERENA out from behind the doorway. SERENA, a twelve-year-old African American girl, has large breasts for her age, and she carries herself with shame.)*

AMANDA: Are you hurt, Serena? *(SERENA doesn't say anything.)*

JOAN: We went to the Nurse's Office, but she said Serena had to go back to class.

AMANDA: So the nurse didn't think she was hurt?

JOAN: She doesn't want to go back to class.

AMANDA: I see. Serena, why don't you come in here for a minute, and we'll talk about this. *(SERENA doesn't budge.)*

JOAN: Come on, Serena. It's okay. *(The two girls enter and sit on the sofa. Neither of them has ever been in the teachers' lounge before, and they are very uncomfortable. AMANDA sits facing them.)*

AMANDA: So, these boys were teasing you—

JOAN: They tried to pull down her pants.

AMANDA: I understand that. Serena, you've been having a lot of trouble with boys this year, haven't you?

JOAN: It's their fault! They're always saying stuff about her breasts, and grabbing at her bra. They make these cow noises when she says anything in class, and they follow her in the hall.

AMANDA: I understand. But you're not physically hurt…

JOAN: She doesn't want to go back to class.

AMANDA: Joan, I appreciate how loyal you are, but Serena needs to speak for herself. *(Turning to the girl.)* So… We've got a problem with boys being boys…

DANA: *(In disbelief.)* She was assaulted!

AMANDA: I think that's kind of a strong word to use for children teasing their classmate.

DANA: They weren't teasing her. They assaulted her.

AMANDA: Dana, I need to ask you to let me handle this. I'm sure you would not appreciate me trying to coach your players in the middle of a game.

DANA: This isn't a game.

AMANDA: I understand that. Now, let me do my job, please. *(DANA sits.)*

So, we can do several things in a case like this. I'm going to outline some of these choices, and I want you to tell me which one you would like best. Okay? *(SERENA nods.)* Now, I can take down the names of all the boys who bothered you, and I can send that to the principal's office, and he can send them all home with a note to the parents.

JOAN: Yeah!

AMANDA: Wait a minute, Joan. And then those boys are all going to say they didn't do it, and that Serena's making it up, and some of the parents are going to get very upset, and then Serena is going to have to go and tell her story to the principal, maybe even in front of the boys and their parents, and they are going to ask her a lot of questions…

JOAN: That's not fair!

AMANDA: And then, do you think those boys are going to be any nicer to Serena after all that, or do you think they're going to act worse?

JOAN: But—

AMANDA: Serena, what do you think? *(SERENA looks down in shame.)*

JOAN: *I* can talk to the principal. I can tell them what happened. I was there. I saw everything that happened!

AMANDA: And do you think that's going to make a difference in how the boys feel about Serena?

DANA: *(Exploding.)* Who cares how the boys feel about Serena? This girl has been attacked by a gang of boys—

AMANDA: It wasn't a "gang." Dana, this kind of heated rhetoric does nothing but create divisions—

DANA: You've got boys trying to tear the clothes off a girl, and you don't think you have divisions!

AMANDA: Girls, we're going to need to finish this discussion in my office. *(She rises. Just then VICTORIA enters.)*

VICTORIA: What are these students doing in the Teachers' Lounge?

AMANDA: We had a situation come up that called for a little on-the-spot girl talk. But we're going to move to my office.

VICTORIA: What happened?

AMANDA: Well, it seems there was a little incident of harassment.

JOAN: They pushed Serena down the stairs and tried to pull her pants down. *(SERENA nudges JOAN to make her stop. They continue to interact in mime.)*

VICTORIA: *(A quick look at DANA.)* I see.

AMANDA: *(An arm around SERENA.)* And I am making the point that no matter what the school does, the real issue for Serena is going to be how she chooses to respond, because she's the one who is going to have to sit in class with those boys every day. And I want her to understand how staying out of class, like she's doing now, is just exactly what that kind of behavior is designed to make her do. But if she goes back there with her head up and a smile on her face—*(SERENA smiles, and AMANDA acknowledges it.)*... and lets those boys know that she's not going to let them bother her—

DANA: That is just bullshit!

AMANDA: *(To VICTORIA.)* Well, we're going to my office. Excuse us. *(She exits with the girls.)*

DANA: I can't believe it! That girl was sexually assaulted in broad daylight in the halls of her school, with a witness, and the guidance counselor is talking to her about her attitude! What kind of shit is that? Those boys should all be expelled.

VICTORIA: It may turn out to be appropriate to *suspend* them, but this is a public institution and before we can take any step like that, we need to look into all the ramifications. Publicity and lawsuits are tremendously destructive—and not just to the administrators, but to the whole community, and, unfortunately, most of all, to the girl herself. Right now Amanda is just focused on Serena, and getting her through the day.

DANA: Getting her through her day? What kind of day can she have? She was assaulted. The day is gone. What are you going to do about the next day and the next! This is just bullshit. And what about all the girls who saw it happen?

VICTORIA: What about those girls? Do you think they're going to report an incident if it ends up with their name in the newspaper and their parents fired from their jobs? Dana, you have never worked in a school system before, and I think it is just a little out of line for you to be telling us all about our business in your first half-hour here. And there's something else I need to warn you about. The kind of language you are throwing around, like "sexual assault" is going to raise a lot of eyebrows. These are children going through adolescence, and there is a lot of sexual tension in these halls. The boys aren't the only ones who are acting out. And when you come in and start using these loaded terms, a lot of people, myself included, are going to wonder if you're someone we want to have around our children, and especially around the boys. And, like it or not, as an unmarried woman your remarks are going to be seen in a different light. As I said, we have not had a problem with gay teachers, but that's not to say there isn't plenty of homophobia around, because there is. I would think twice before I said anything that would give anyone ammunition.

DANA: They were pulling down her underwear!

VICTORIA: All right, Dana. That's all I'm going to say. And I will be looking into the incident. We have a detailed procedure for handling situations like this.

DANA: I can see that.

VICTORIA: Now, if you'll excuse me, I'm going to talk to the girls. *(She is just starting to leave when the NURSE bursts in. VICTORIA is intimidated by her.)*

NURSE: What are those girls doing with Amanda? I sent them back to class.

VICTORIA: I'm going to meet with them right now.

NURSE: Well, there's nothing wrong with that black girl. I had a look at her. Nothing wrong. I think she and her little friend are just trying to get out of class.

VICTORIA: Well, Serena seems to be upset.

NURSE: No doubt. I sent her back to class. Does Amanda know I did that?

VICTORIA: I'll ask her.

DANA: She knows.

NURSE: *(Noticing DANA for the first time.)* Well, they're just using her.

VICTORIA: Yes, excuse me. *(She exits.)*

NURSE: *(To DANA.)* You talked to them?

DANA: They came in here.

NURSE: *(Shaking her head.)* Well, I sent them back to class.

DANA: You didn't believe them?

NURSE: What? That the girl fell down and the boys were trying to look at her underpants?

DANA: That she was *assaulted.*

NURSE: What?

DANA: She was assaulted.

NURSE: You were there?

DANA: No, but that's what she described.

NURSE: Who are you?

DANA: The new P.E. teacher. Dana Willetts.

NURSE: Well, let me tell you something, Miss Willetts…

DANA: Ms. Willetts.

NURSE: Do you call it an assault every time one of your basketball players knocks another girl down?

DANA: I call it a foul. And it's part of the game.

NURSE: And this was part of the game. And I'll tell you another part of the game. It's called playing the staff off against the faculty. Like the way those girls went hunting up the guidance counselor when they couldn't get what they wanted from me.

DANA: Those girls went looking for someone who could help them, because you didn't.

NURSE: Well, I can see you're going to be sending me half your class every P.E. period. You know the girls will say anything to get out of P.E., don't you?

DANA: I don't know that.

NURSE: Well, they will. *(Just then ANNE enters, carrying a purse. She is very nervous and distracted, on the brink of a breakdown. She crosses quietly to the sofa and sits on the cushion under which the gun was found. She does not notice DANA, whose back is to her. The NURSE turns to her.)* Isn't that right?

ANNE: *(Distracted.)* What?

NURSE: The girls will use any excuse to get out of going to P.E. *(ANNE, feeling under the cushion, does not look up.)* Well?

ANNE: *(ANNE's head is still down. DANA, who has recognized ANNE, is staring at her.)* Oh, I don't know.

NURSE: *(To DANA.)* Well, they will. And I'm going to tell you now, I'm going to send them all right back to class, just like that little Black girl. Right back. *(DANA, still staring at ANNE, doesn't acknowledge the threat, and the NURSE, disgusted, turns and exits. ANNE is still feeling under the cushion and down the cracks of the sofa, looking for the gun. She has not noticed DANA. DANA crosses to the sofa and stands in front of her.)*

DANA: Anne? *(ANNE looks up with a start. The two women look at each other.)* So, how are you? It's been a long time. *(ANNE rises abruptly and awkwardly.)* They didn't tell you I was the new P.E. teacher?

ANNE: *(A worried parting look in the direction of the sofa cushion.)* No. It's… kind of a shock.

DANA: You teach here?

ANNE: English.

DANA: So, should we just pretend we don't know each other?

ANNE: Oh, no. You don't need to do that. I mean, I don't see anything wrong with the fact we were college roommates.

DANA: I don't see anything wrong with the rest of it. *(Embarrassed, ANNE looks away.)* Are you married?

ANNE: Yes. Two daughters. And you?

DANA: Am *I* married?

ANNE: *(Brief pause.)* With a partner…?

DANA: Not at the moment. *(An awkward pause.)*

ANNE: Dana, I was so young… I didn't know what I was doing.

DANA: *(Smiling.)* Are you referring to the husband or to us.

ANNE: *(Smiling.)* To us. I'm not a lesbian.

DANA: Mmmm. Passing phase?

ANNE: You were persuasive.

DANA: But not enough. *(ANNE laughs.)* So how have you been? It's been… fifteen years?

ANNE: Well. You know I got a Masters degree in English.

DANA: Creative Writing.

ANNE: You have a better memory than I do.

DANA: You made quite an impression on me. So did you write creatively?

ANNE: Oh, a little. But I was pregnant my last term.

DANA: The husband?

ANNE: No. Actually, I didn't marry Dana's father.

DANA: "Dana?"

ANNE: I named the first after you.

DANA: *(Moved.)* Why didn't you tell me? *(ANNE shrugs.)* You know I got on a pro basketball team. One of the first.

ANNE: No, I didn't know. But I'm not surprised. You were a great athlete.

DANA: Are.

ANNE: Are. Sorry. And what about you? You played pro ball…

DANA: Did some coaching, did some traveling. Sowed some wild oats. What'd you name the second one?

ANNE: Cristina.

DANA: A girlfriend on the side?

ANNE: After my mother.

DANA: I'd like to see your girls.

ANNE: I… They don't live with me. They're with their father in Michigan.

DANA: Oh.

ANNE: I… It… just worked out better.

DANA: Anne, are you all right?

ANNE: No. No, I'm not, but it's all right.

DANA: *(Watching ANNE closely.)* That wouldn't by any chance have been your gun under the cushion there?

ANNE: You found it?

DANA: Victoria found it.

ANNE: Oh, no. Did she take it?

DANA: It's in the cabinet.

ANNE: Where? *(DANA points, and ANNE crosses hurriedly to it.)* Don't tell. *(She takes the gun and puts it in her purse.)*

DANA: What are you doing with a gun?

ANNE: I found it in one of the boys' desks. I didn't have my purse with me, so I wrapped it in my sweater and hid it in the sofa.

DANA: Why didn't you turn it in to the office?

ANNE: *(Embarrassed.)* I… I need a gun.

DANA: Why? *(ANNE doesn't say anything.)* Anne, do you know why the P.E. teacher was fired?

ANNE: *(Quickly.)* She resigned.

DANA: She was fired.

ANNE: They told us she resigned.

DANA: Okay. So why did she resign?

ANNE: They didn't tell us.

DANA: But you must have heard the rumors.

ANNE: The rumors aren't true.

DANA: How do you know?

ANNE: Because I knew Barbara. Dana, don't ask me any more about it.

DANA: Why not?

ANNE: Just don't. You don't understand what it's like here. You're not going to fit. It's…

DANA: It's what?

ANNE: Different. It's just different. Please don't ask me any more.

DANA: Did they fire her because she was lesbian?

ANNE: I told you I don't want to talk about it.

DANA: Well, did they?

ANNE: Don't ask me any more about it!

DANA: Anne, tell me. *(She takes her arm.)*

ANNE: Let go of me. *(VICTORIA and AMANDA enter.)* I don't know why Barbara resigned. I don't know.

VICTORIA: What's going on here?

DANA: Anne and I were discussing why Barbara was fired.

ANNE: I told you she resigned. I told you I don't know anything about it.

DANA: No, that's not what you told me. You told me not to ask. *(To VICTORIA.)* I want to know why I'm not supposed to ask.

ANNE: I have to go. *(She exits.)*

VICTORIA: So, you know Anne?

DANA: We were roommates in college.

VICTORIA: Ah. Then you know about her problem?

DANA: Her problem?

VICTORIA: Her mental illness.

AMANDA: She was out for two months this winter.

DANA: So you're saying I shouldn't believe her?

VICTORIA: I'm not saying that.

DANA: What are you saying?

VICTORIA: She's very unstable right now. *(Lowering her voice.)* I'm afraid we won't be renewing her contract for next year.

ANNE: *(Appearing in the doorway.)* I heard that!

VICTORIA: *(Surprised.)* Anne…

ANNE: You're going to fire me!

VICTORIA: Were you eavesdropping?

ANNE: There's *nothing* wrong with my teaching! *(To DANA.)* Nothing! *(To VICTORIA.)* You can ask my students.

VICTORIA: I'm sure there's nothing wrong.

ANNE: Then why would you fire me?

VICTORIA: Well, Anne, this wouldn't be the time or place I would choose for having this discussion.

ANNE: If I'm a good teacher, why would you fire me?

VICTORIA: Because of behaviors like this.

ANNE: Like what?

VICTORIA: Spying on your colleagues and creating a scene.

ANNE: You were lying about me behind my back!

AMANDA: *(Reaching toward ANNE.)* Have you taken your meds today?

ANNE: *(Backing away.)* That's none of your business! Dana, you see? This is what I was trying to tell you.

DANA: What?

ANNE: This! What they're doing right now to me!

VICTORIA: Nobody's doing anything to you.

ANNE: This is exactly what they did to Barbara, only worse, because she was lesbian—

VICTORIA: What are you talking about?

ANNE: *(To DANA.)* They set her up. And all the students knew it, too. They knew they could get away with anything, and that's why they attacked her.

VICTORIA: *Who* attacked her?

ANNE: *(To DANA.)* Some of the football players attacked her after a game. *(To VICTORIA.)* Yes, they did. You know they did. And when she tried to report it, the school acted like it was her fault, because she had spoken up about the way the boys' athletic program was funded. And they said they would investigate, but instead of investigating the boys who attacked her, they investigated *her*! And then, of course, she resigned, just like you knew she would.

AMANDA: *(An arm on ANNE.)* Anne, I think you should calm down.

ANNE: *(Dangerous.)* I think you should stop touching me. I think you should stop touching everyone, Ms. Touchy-Feely. That's what they call you. Nobody likes it. They know it's phoney. *(To DANA.)* If a girl gets called a bitch or a whore, she gets a pat on the head. If she's been shoved up against a locker and had her shirt pulled up, she gets an arm around her shoulder. That's what she does. She touches you. That's her job. Don't touch me! *(During this speech, RUDY has come to the door, and VICTORIA has spoken quietly to him.)* I told Dana she wouldn't fit in here—*(To DANA.)* Didn't I? *(To the others.)* And she's not. You don't know Dana, or you wouldn't have hired her, but she's not like you. She's not going to stand around and let the girls get treated like shit, mauled in the halls and ignored in the classrooms, while the boys get away with murder. She's going to get up in your face about it. And she's not going to go away without a fight, either, because Dana is a fighter. She fights for what she believes in. She's not like me, or like Barbara. You're not going to be able to scare her. *(The NURSE appears at the door with RUDY. VICTORIA whispers to her. ANNE sees this.)* What? What is *she* doing here? What are you saying? *(The NURSE advances.)* Don't touch me! Don't come any closer! *(She pulls the gun out of her purse as she backs toward the door.)* Don't come near me. Don't! I have a gun! I have a gun! *(RUDY grabs her from behind, and ANNE drops the gun on the floor. She wrestles a little and then begins to sob.)* Dana! Dana! Help me! Help me! *(The NURSE crosses to RUDY.)*

VICTORIA: *(To the NURSE, in a low voice.)* Call her husband.

ANNE: No! No! Not him! Don't call him! He hates me! He's trying to kill me! *(Whimpering.)* He's trying to kill me…

VICTORIA: Anne, your husband loves you. He wants to see you well again, and so do we. *(She is weeping as the NURSE and RUDY lead her out of the teachers' lounge. There is a moment of silence.)*

VICTORIA: *(To DANA.)* You showed her where the gun was? *(DANA says nothing. VICTORIA gets a napkin and crosses to pick up the gun. DANA puts her foot on it.)*

DANA: Don't.

VICTORIA: What?

DANA: Don't touch up that gun.

VICTORIA: It's contraband. I need to turn it in to the office.

DANA: *(Her foot still on the gun.)* That's not what you're going to do with it. You're going to turn it in to the police, because Anne's fingerprints are on it. You're going to say that she threatened you with it.

VICTORIA: She *did* threaten me with it, and there were several witnesses.

DANA: You want to see her locked up.

VICTORIA: Yes, I do. She's dangerous. *(She looks at DANA and then reaches again for the gun.)*

DANA: Don't touch that gun. *(Suddenly AMANDA shoves DANA. DANA loses her balance for a second, and AMANDA lunges for the gun. DANA manages to get her foot back on it, but AMANDA tries to pull it away. DANA's hands are not touching the gun at all when it goes off, shooting AMANDA in the face. She dies instantly. Both women back away in horror. After a long moment, DANA and VICTORIA look at each other. Slowly DANA reaches for the gun. Taking it, she points it at VICTORIA.)*

DANA: Put your hands over your head. *(VICTORIA does.)* Lie down on the floor. *(VICTORIA kneels.)* Face down. *(She lies down.)* I'm going to go out to my car now, and I can see into the teachers' lounge from the parking lot. If I see you get up, I'm going to shoot. Do you understand? Nod your head if you understand. *(VICTORIA nods. DANA backs out of the room, closing the door after her. VICTORIA lies still. There is the sound of a car door opening and closing, and an engine starting. The car is heard driving off. VICTORIA rises cautiously, looks out the window, and then crosses to the phone. She dials "911.")*

VICTORIA: Hello? There's been a murder at Rosa Parks Middle School. A teacher has been shot... *(A pause.)* Yes. Yes, I do... It was the PE teacher.

Blackout

End of Play

The Gage and Mr. Comstock

A Play in One Act

*This play is dedicated to Fae Jolie-ge Silverman,
my unfailingly honest critic and friend.*

The Gage and Mr. Comstock

A Play in One Act

Formidable 19th century feminist activist and Suffragist Matilda Joslyn Gage, 67, lies in bed, demoralized and debilitated following the publication of a book that marks the culmination of her lifework: *Woman, Church, and State.*

Her book, an impeccably researched, comprehensive indictment of the historical misogyny of the Christian church, is intended to start a revolution, but, so far, all she is receiving are congratulatory notes from her supporters. Gage's exhaustion, however, changes to exhilaration when she comes across a letter from Anthony Comstock, the notorious, self-appointed censor who authored the infamous "Comstock Laws" banning birth control .

Gage, delighted that Comstock is attempting to censor her book, gleefully anticipates the controversy of the coming campaign.

One female
Ten minutes
Single set

Cast of Characters

MATILDA JOSLYN GAGE: A woman, 67.

Scene
Gage's bedroom in her home in Fayetteville, NY.

Time
August 1893.

The Gage and Mr. Comstock

The bedroom of MATILDA JOSLYN GAGE, Fayetteville, New York. It is an afternoon in August 1893. MATILDA GAGE, 67, lies in the bed, surrounded by a stack of unopened letters. Her nightstand is piled with newspapers, books, and more letters. She is engaged in tearing up the letters and throwing them around the room.

GAGE: *(Reading from a letter.)* "Meticulous attention to detail..." blah blah blah... "The obvious intelligence of the with which it was crafted..." *(With a cry of exasperation, she rips up the letter and throws it on the floor. She begins to rip up all the letters and hurl them on the floor.)* Don't... bring... me... any... more... of... these... damned... get-well... hope-you're-feeling-better... congratulations-on-your-new-book... letters! *(Exhausted, she falls back on her pillows.)* Yes, I'm tired. I'm exhausted. And, yes, I have "taken to my bed..." But it is *not* from finishing my book. It's because of *these... damned... well wishers*! *(Indicating the letters on the floor.)*

You don't know who I am, do you? *(She laughs.)* Of course you don't. I'll bet you know Susan B. Anthony... If nothing else, she's got her profile on the dollar. And Elizabeth Cady Stanton? Yes, you've heard of her at least. But I'll bet you've never heard of Matilda Joslyn Gage, have you? Well, there were three of us, like the Musketeers... Elizabeth, Susan, and I shared the leadership of the National Women's Suffrage Association. We wrote the *History of Women's Suffrage* together. I edited the paper for the movement. But you've never heard of me. Such is the fate of the woman who refuses to compromise. *(She sighs.)* And it would then go without saying that you had never heard of my book either—*Woman, Church, and State* ...? There's probably even a copy of it in your public library—a sure sign of obscurity. Oh, if I could just get it banned... One good banning is worth a hundred of these... *(Indicating the letters.)* ... a million of these! *(She leans back.)*

Not that I haven't tried. Last month, I donated a copy to the local school library here in Fayetteville. I sent it to the most conservative member of the school board, Mr. Thomas W. Sheedy. The least Mr. Sheedy could do is send it back to me, with a courteous, but firm note about the unsuitability of the material for children. *(Sighing.)* But he is choosing to ignore my book. Perhaps he has even sent it on to the school library. What an ideal burial ground for a radical book... a book that dares to claim that the Christian church—that all Christian churches—are founded on the notion that woman was created inferior and secondary to man and that she was, and continues to be, the agent of original sin, causing men—poor, innocent dears—to be tempted and to fall from their Father's grace. No mention of a mother, of course. Well... what do you expect from a theology that espouses—and I mean that literally—"immaculate conception?" And *that* book—you know the one I'm talking about—that antiquarian fount of monumental disinformation—is found in every parlor in America, while *my* book—my book with a mission no more ambitious than to state the obvious—namely, that *every* church is the enemy of liberty and progress and the chief means of enslaving women's conscience and reason—is relegated, not even to the honest dignity of the dust heap, but to that mausoleum of respectability—the school library!

Do you know what a gage is? I'm not talking about myself. I mean the noun. A gage. G-a-g-e. *(Pausing.)* It's the glove a person throws down when they want to challenge someone to a duel. And if the other person picks up the gage, that is the sign that they are pledged to combat. And then, of course, it is a fight to the death. That is the point of a duel. There can be only one winner... or none at all, if they both die. But, in either case, there is a resolution. The demand for the *opportunity to* avenge a wrong has been satisfied.

But let us say that a woman has thrown down the glove. Ah. A *woman.* Well, she must have dropped it, of course, by accident... or perhaps it is a flirtatious gesture. Who can tell? And woman, capricious as she is, would she herself even know? And so the person who bends down to retrieve it is merely executing a perfunctory act of common courtesy. It is not a gage at all, but merely a glove. *(Becoming increasingly incensed.)* The chivalrous picker-upper of the glove may even note in passing the "workmanship" of it... its "meticulous attention to detail" or "the obvious intelligence with which it was crafted..." *(She hurls her book to the floor.)*

This is my gage! There! Don't touch it! Leave it right there... leave it right there in the middle of the floor, unless you understand what it means to pick it up. Unless you understand that this is a challenge, a duel that can have only one winner. Don't you dare pick it up, leaf through it, or even read it and then send me one of these... *(Grabbing a new handful of letters.)* ... these epistolary pats on the head... *(She resumes shredding and hurling the notes.)* ... these manumitted little wolves in sheep's clothing... these premature obituaries... these—*(She stops abruptly, her eye caught by the return address on one of the envelopes.)* Oh... *(She opens it.)* Oh! *(She scans it.)* Well, now here is something different. Well... yes... It appears that Mr. Sheedy did read my book after all... *(She reads it.)* Yes... indeed... *(She looks up.)*

This is from Mr. Comstock. You know who he is, don't you? If you don't, you should. He's probably responsible for half of you being here today. He banned contraception, you know. And it wasn't until 1960 that birth control was made legal in this country. Those Comstock laws would have been in place for some of your parents and most of your grandparents.

Who is Mr. Comstock? I am sorry to say that he is a mentally and morally unbalanced man, who does not know right from wrong or the facts of history from "tales of lust." A fool who is a press censor is more to be feared than a knave, and Comstock seems to be both a fool and a knave. Buddha declared the only sin to be ignorance, and if this be true, then Anthony Comstock is a great sinner.

He formed the New York Society for the Suppression of Vice, and, then he lobbied Congress tirelessly, until, in 1873, he succeeded in getting them to pass the "Act of the Suppression of Trade in, and Circulation of, Obscene Literature and Articles of Immoral Use," more affectionately known as "The Comstock Law." Quite a campaign. Yes... I will never forget their slogan... "Morals, not art and literature."

For the last twenty years, this man has been working as a special, unpaid postal inspector, with the power to enter any post office and confiscate any material he deems obscene. So far, he has been responsible for the burning of more than a hundred tons of literature, a record that, I believe, surpasses the burning of the great library at Alexandria.

Let's see... He had Walt Whitman fired from the Department of the Interior for writing *Leaves of Grass.* But Mr. Comstock is an equal-opportunity bigot. He had a woman arrested for sending a postcard in which she referred to her husband as a "spitbub"—"spitbub" being an archaic colloquialism for "son of a bitch."

But what is most unforgivable was his treatment of Ann Lohman, otherwise known as Madame Restell. She had performed abortions—yes, she had—and she had been arrested, indicted, tried, sentenced and served her time. But this was not good enough for Mr. Comstock. Oh, no... Shortly after the passage of the Comstock Laws banned the sale of contraceptives, he sent undercover agents to Mrs. Lohman's home, to purchase those so-called "articles of immoral use"—and, who should be more entitled to sell birth control than the woman who had been so intimately involved with the tragedies and complications of women desperate to terminate their unwanted pregnancies—a woman who had served her time in federal prison for attempting to ameliorate the plight of women who, more often than not, had been the victims of rape or incest?

And, yes, Ann Lohman did sell these men the contraceptives they requested, and probably congratulated them on their rare masculine sensitivity to the vulnerabilities of their wives and girlfriends— as would be appropriate! But for this, Mr. Comstock had her re-arrested. And so, in the early morning hours of the day that had been set for her trial, Ann Lohman—with habitual attention to sanitary conditions—climbed into a bathtub filled with water and slit her own throat. Mr. Comstock's callous response to the news was simply, "A bloody ending to a bloody life." *(She holds up the letter.)* And this letter I hold in my hand is from this same Anthony Comstock, self-appointed arbiter of the public's morals. It is Mr. Comstock who has taken up my gage, and I am more than prepared to fight him to the death! *(She unfolds the letter again.)*

He is apparently threatening the school board with arrest if they place my book in the school library: *(Smiling at the audience.)* Goody. *(Reading.)* "The incidents of victims of lust told in this book are such that if I found a person putting that book indiscriminately before the children, I would institute a criminal proceeding against them for doing it." *(She looks up.)* This is the best thing that could have happened. *(Looking around for pen and paper.)* I must get a copy of this to the local paper immediately... and with any luck the Church will pick up the thing and call for suppression of the book. *(Pausing.)* Now, that would be something! To get *Woman, Church, and State* in the "Index Expurgatorious"—the Pope's list of banned books! *(She reaches for pen and paper and begins to write furiously. Pausing abruptly, she looks up.)*

I'm sorry... I'm being rude... But there's so much to do. Here... Would one of you like to take this copy home? *(A pause.)* Well, come on... Isn't there anyone here brave enough to take up the gage? *(A pause.)* Be careful! They might arrest you, you know. *(Winking conspiratorially, she turns away from the audience back to her writing.)*

Blackout

End of Play

www.ingramcontent.com/pod-product-compliance
Lightning Source LLC
Chambersburg PA
CBHW022250290526
45785CB00015B/486